tters

# Working in Policing

Policing Matters

# Working in Policing

Edited by Ian K. Pepper

LearningMatters

First published in 2011 by Learning Matters Ltd

*British Library Cataloguing in Publication Data*
A CIP record for this book is available from the British Library.

ISBN: 978 0 85725 489 4

This book is also available in the following ebook formats:

Adobe ebook    ISBN: 978 0 85725 491 7
EPUB ebook     ISBN: 978 0 85725 490 0
Kindle         ISBN: 978 0 85725 492 4

Cover and text design by Toucan Design
Project Management by Newgen Publishing and Data Services
Typeset by Newgen Publishing and Data Services
Printed and bound in Great Britain by Short Run Press Ltd, Exeter, Devon

Learning Matters Ltd
20 Cathedral Yard
Exeter EX1 1HB
Tel: 01392 215560
info@learningmatters.co.uk
www.learningmatters.co.uk

All weblinks and web addresses in this book have been carefully checked prior to publication, but for up-to-date information please visit the Learning Matters website, www.learningmatters.co.uk.

FSC
www.fsc.org
MIX
Paper from
responsible sources
FSC® C014540

# Contents

# Contributors

**Christopher Blake** is a Principal Lecturer at Teesside University responsible for the management and delivery of a collaborative policing programme for student police officers with West Mercia Police. Christopher worked for West Midlands Police for thirty years in uniformed operations specialising in roads policing and staff training and development. While seconded to the Central Police Training and Development Authority he worked both as a team leader and as a training manager. Christopher has also delivered investigative training to detectives in Rwanda.

**Ruth McGrath** is a Senior Lecturer in Law and Policing at Teesside University, teaching on a range of vocationally focused policing programmes with partner organisations. She is a former police sergeant with Cleveland Police and has experience across a broad range of policing specialisms, including roads policing, criminal investigation and police custody. As a former police trainer she had responsibility for training and development of staff at all levels of the organisation, and continues to be involved in the recruitment and assessment process for potential police and community support officers.

**Helen Pepper** is a Senior Lecturer in Police Studies at Teesside University leading the delivery of a 'Skillsmark' endorsed Foundation Degree in Police Studies in partnership with Cleveland Police. Helen started her career with the Forensic Science Service as an assistant scientific officer. She later moved on to become a crime scene investigator (CSI) with West Yorkshire Police. She has been a senior scientific support officer with Durham Constabulary and the force forensic trainer. Helen has also been the acting Head of the Durham Constabulary Crime Scene Investigation Department.

**Ian K. Pepper** is the Principal Lecturer in Policing at Teesside University, UK. Ian manages and teaches on a range of education and training programmes in partnership with numerous law enforcement organisations. He is a former Senior Lecturer in Crime Scene and Forensic Science, police crime scene investigator (CSI) and fingerprint officer with West Yorkshire Police. Ian has been an instructor and team leader at the National Training Centre for Scientific Support to Crime Investigation and has designed and delivered training to Police Officers and Crime Scene Investigators worldwide. He is a member of the International Association for Identification, the Fingerprint Society and the Higher Education Academy.

**Samantha Scott** is a Senior Lecturer in Policing, Investigation and Law at Teesside University. She currently teaches on a range of policing programmes, as well as undergraduate, postgraduate and online courses. Samantha began her policing career with Cleveland Police as an Emergency Control Room Operator. She later trained in crime scene examination and also serious and organised crime. Samantha is a member of the International Investigative Interviewing Research Group (iIIRG) and the Fingerprint Society.

**Barrie Sheldon** is a Senior Lecturer at Teesside University delivering a foundation degree in policing to West Mercia Police student police officers and online programmes in counter-terrorism. Barrie joined Staffordshire Police as a cadet in 1972 and retired in 2004. He enjoyed various operational roles and completed his career with the Major Investigation Department as a Senior Investigating Officer. Barrie was also involved with training during his policing career and has also delivered investigative training to detectives in Rwanda.

**Rachael Strzelecki** is a Senior Lecturer in Policing at Teesside University teaching a Foundation Degree in Professional Policing in partnership with West Mercia Police. She also delivers online programmes on the uses of intelligence. Rachael started her career as a Crime and Intelligence Analyst with Cleveland Police before moving on to become a Qualitative Research Analyst.

**Peter Williams** is a Senior Lecturer with Teesside University teaching programmes in partnership with West Mercia Police and the military police, as well as delivering online programmes in counter-terrorism. Peter served thirty years with Merseyside Police and retired as a police Inspector, having also served as a custody officer and trainer in the force custody department along with performing a consultative role for custody matters with the police in Hungary. Prior to his operational police career Peter worked as a member of police staff with the then Liverpool and Bootle Constabulary and served in the Royal Air Force Police.

# Introduction and context

IAN K. PEPPER

## An introduction to working in policing

The whole criminal justice system across the United Kingdom employs more than 500,000 people (Skills for Justice, 2009) and includes the police and other protective services such as the Border Agency, courts and crown prosecution services, prison service, probation service and victim support services.

Of the 500,000, over 244,000 people are directly employed across the police service in England and Wales (Home Office, 2010a), completing a vast array of fascinating and intriguing roles to support the needs of modern policing. Research conducted by Pepper and McGrath (2010) suggests that many people who are interested in working within the police service may be unaware of or have not considered the range of career opportunities available to them. Often people's perceptions of various policing roles are also influenced by what is portrayed in the media. This is no more evident than in what has become known as the 'CSI effect', describing the degree to which the general public has raised expectations of forensic evidence in the investigation of crime and is attributed to the popular television series 'CSI'. Research conducted by Stinson et al. (2007) also supports this view.

The careers available within policing are many and definitely varied. Skills for Justice (2009) identified that about 57 per cent of the whole justice sector's workforce are employed in policing and the associated protective services, with Donnelly and Scott (2008) suggesting that one-third of police employees across Scotland are police staff rather than police officers. Both the uniformed and non-uniformed roles of the police officer can range from being a neighbourhood police officer engaging with the local community to a non-uniformed detective working as a special branch officer gathering information and intelligence. These police officer roles are supplemented by other uniformed operational roles such as community support officers and part-time police officers known as 'special constables'. For a number of years, civilians have also been recruited into police staff roles to support operational policing. These initiatives grew significantly as a result of a circular released to police forces by the Home Office (1988) which identified the benefits of increased civilian recruitment releasing police officers for operational roles. This recruitment has further evolved as a result of the twenty-first century workforce modernisation initiatives. Examples of civilian, now termed 'police staff', roles within policing fall into two distinct categories, those which require specific qualifications, experience and training before employment and those which require aptitude and ability with training being conducted by the police service at a local, force, regional or national level.

An example of a role which would require specific qualifications, experience and training prior to employment would be that of a force accountant, where an applicant would need to be a fully qualified accountant who could prove that they had experience of working in accounting and/or a financial services role within another organisation as they would be dealing with, and responsible for, public money. A HOLMES (Home Office Large Major Enquiry System) indexer, however, would have to be able to demonstrate at assessment and interview that they could handle large numbers of incoming telephone calls, use information technology and type and proofread documents together with gathering and disseminating information from briefings. Once employed and trained, HOLMES indexers provide an efficient and effective administrative support role for major incident rooms which would include the preparation, research and maintenance of the HOLMES computer databases.

However, nationally, there are inconsistencies across the police forces in respect of professional titles, roles and responsibilities of those who are employed in specific tasks. For example, a scientific support manager (who could be a senior police officer or senior member of the police staff) in some police forces may be called the Head of Forensic Services or Forensic Investigation (or some other title). They would normally be responsible for the strategic management of the crime scene investigation department, fingerprint bureau, imaging department and chemical enhancement laboratory, but in some police forces, they may also be responsible for a host of other activities such as DNA submissions, a hi-tech crime unit or a footwear comparison department.

The opportunities for recruitment as a police officer, community support officer or special constable across England and Wales are advertised nationally through the police service recruitment gateway at www.policecouldyou.co.uk/. Police officer recruitment in Scotland, Northern Ireland and other police forces is advertised through the individual forces' websites. However, at the time of writing, several police forces across Scotland are piloting a central recruitment process. Police staff roles across all forces are advertised both locally through force websites and local newspapers and nationally through recruitment websites and police publications.

Other law enforcement agencies also provide specific policing and security roles which are not included in the list of police forces in the Appendix on pages 151–153, such as the Belfast International Airport Constabulary, the Port of Dover Police and the Mersey Tunnels Police.

Opportunities also exist within a number of police forces to be an unpaid volunteer for several hours each week assisting in the running of police stations with administrative duties or supporting witnesses. For those between 16 and 18 years of age (occasionally from the age of 14), several police forces run a police cadet scheme, where unpaid but uniformed cadets gain training in and experience of the police service. Cadets learn police procedures and criminal law, team working and first aid skills, and can perform non-confrontational tasks such as crime reduction initiatives.

During 2010, the majority of police forces across the United Kingdom suspended recruitment of police officers, and for the most part police staff, for an indeterminable length of time, were subject to financial reviews within the police forces themselves. This is due to each force having their central government funding reduced by 4 per cent a year between the financial years 2010–11 and 2014–15. A number of other law enforcement agencies, such as the National Police Improvement Agency and the Serious Organised Crime Agency, have also been notified of their impending re-organisation and re-branding. The police service as a whole, both police officers and police staff, has also been subject to a review of both pay and conditions of service (Winsor, 2011).

However, in these times of change, the special constabulary and other voluntary roles continue to recruit and are set to expand significantly (Home Office, 2010b). Some police forces, such as the Metropolitan Police Service (Metropolitan Police, 2010), are also considering using the special constabulary as an entry route to becoming a regular police officer. A number of the non-Home Office police forces, such as the Civil Nuclear Constabulary (CNC) and the British Transport Police, also continue to recruit either police officers or police staff from time to time.

There are also a number of universities and further education colleges which are now delivering 'pre-join' programmes, often in partnership with their local police force. Such courses range from short courses of study to full degrees, enabling individuals who are interested in a career within policing to become conversant with some of the knowledge and skills required for specific job roles within the police family. This in turn would place them in a favourable position once recruitment of police officers and staff inevitably recommences.

# About this book

The role of the police officer is essential for the effective delivery of modern policing, but there are also many other roles defined by HMIC (2011) as front line (visible or specialist), middle office or back office of which people are unaware, where individuals are employed by the police service to ensure policing is delivered effectively 365 days a year, 24 hours a day.

This book is written by those who have experienced such policing first hand across seven different police forces and national policing organisations working both day and night on the front line or middle office performing operational, visible or specialist policing tasks supporting the role of contemporary policing. The text guides those interested in either working within the police or interested in how the police work through 22 career opportunities available, as listed in the following table, within the contemporary police service, although many more roles exist.

*Policing roles covered within this book*

| Career opportunity | Chapter | Police role, HMIC (2011) |
|---|---|---|
| Call taker | 1 | Middle office |
| Control room dispatcher | 1 | Middle office |
| Police officer | 2 | Front line (visible or specialist) |
| Community support officer | 2 | Front line (visible or specialist) |
| Special constable | 2 | Front line (visible or specialist) |
| Crime scene investigator | 3 | Front line (visible or specialist) |
| Fingerprint examiner | 3 | Front line (visible or specialist) |
| Chemical enhancement technician | 3 | Front line (visible or specialist) |
| Forensic photographer | 3 | Front line (visible or specialist) |
| Forensic computer analyst | 3 | Front line (visible or specialist) |
| Police detective (constable) | 4 | Front line (visible or specialist) |
| Police staff investigator (civilian) | 4 | Front line (visible or specialist) |
| Intelligence analyst | 5 | Middle office |
| Geographic and behavioural profiler | 5 | Middle office |
| Road Policing Unit officer | 6 | Front line (visible or specialist) |
| ANPR operator | 6 | Middle office |
| Road death/collision investigator | 6 | Front line (visible or specialist) |
| Authorised firearms officer | 6 | Front line (visible or specialist) |
| Custody officer | 7 | Middle office |
| Lay visitors (or custody visitors) | 7 | Additional voluntary role |
| Detention officer/custody assistant | 7 | Middle office |
| Case management officer | 7 | Middle office |

# The context of modern policing

The police service of the United Kingdom consists of 43 police forces across England and Wales from Northumbria Police in the north-east of England, Devon and Cornwall Police in the south-west, Norfolk Constabulary in the east and North Wales Police in the west. There are eight police forces in Scotland such as the Northern Constabulary which polices the Highlands and Islands of Scotland and the Police Service of Northern Ireland which has responsibility for policing this geographical area. There are also a number of other policing agencies with specific roles and responsibilities ranging from the Ministry of Defence Police and CNC to the States of Jersey Police and the Royal Gibraltar Police.

The foundations for this modern police service were laid in the first half of the nineteenth century when the home secretary of the time, Sir Robert Peel, introduced the

Metropolitan Police Act (1829). This Act built on previous law enforcement initiatives such as the Statute of Winchester in 1285 which detailed how every person had a duty to uphold the peace together with the establishment of the part-time role of the constable (Rowe, 2008), and the Fielding brothers' eighteenth-century Bow Street Runners who worked in London to arrest robbers, murderers and highwaymen. The Metropolitan Police Act (1829) established the metropolitan police area which initially extended several miles from central London. This led to a small force of suitable men being recruited and sworn in as police constables (women were not employed by the police service until early in the twentieth century). The 1831 Special Constables Act also enabled local magistrates to conscript men during time of need in order to enforce the law, and the 1835 Municipal Corporation Act formalised the establishment of regular police forces across the rest of England and Wales. Today, the Metropolitan Police Service is the largest police force in the United Kingdom, with an annual budget of £3.6 billion. The service aims to provide effective and safe policing for over seven million people across London (Metropolitan Police Authority and Metropolitan Police Service, 2009). The Metropolitan Police Service hopes to achieve its aims by utilising its workforce of some 32,000 police officers, including 7,000 female officers and 2,735 black and ethnic minority officers (Metropolitan Police Authority and Metropolitan Police Service, 2009) and over 14,000 police staff (Home Office, 2010a), to work together as a team to meet the commissioner's aims of providing a police presence in communities, improving performance and productivity and providing professionalism in terms of personal responsibility and pride in the service (Metropolitan Police Authority and Metropolitan Police Service, 2009).

The governance (or political control and oversight) of the police service across England and Wales is currently split into a 'tripartite system' between the chief constable in each force (or commissioner in the Metropolitan Police), the police authority in each force and the Home Office. This system was first established by the Police Act (1964) with the chief constables having operational autonomy on priorities and policing within their own force area (Rowe, 2008). However, in May 2010, the Government announced plans for a Police Reform and Social Responsibility Bill which will lead, by 2012, to the appointment of elected civilian police commissioners across England and Wales. The commissioners will represent the community served by the force and have greater oversight of all aspects of policing such as setting priorities and budgets. Across Scotland, the 'tripartite system' of governance, established in 1967, is currently shared between the chief constable, the police authority and Scottish ministers (Donnelly and Scott, 2008). In Northern Ireland, oversight and accountability of policing is provided by the Policing Board, District Policing Partnerships and the Police Ombudsman established as a result of recommendations of the 1999 Patten Report (Mulcahy, 2008).

In the twenty-first century, there has been a wholesale shift within the government and the police service across England and Wales to a focus on neighbourhood policing. This has evolved from a problem-orientated policing (POP) approach which had initially been adopted in the 1990s. POP within the United Kingdom was derived from a concept first published in 1979 in the United States. At the root of the concept is the ability of the police to move from dealing just with the crime to dealing with the issues within the community that lead to the crime (Leigh et al., 1996). The idea of working within the community has been further driven by the government programme of 'justice seen, justice done' which responded to a review conducted by Casey (2008) into the engagement of communities in dealing with crime and raising public awareness and confidence in the whole criminal justice system.

Casey (2008) had highlighted significant effects of crime on the community. Nearly three quarters of those surveyed reported that hearing of a crime in their community made them feel both unsafe and cautious. The report also identified possible resolutions, such as the establishment across England and Wales of a local police presence within every neighbourhood to provide standard police services. Flanagan's (2008) review of policing had also identified a need to move to a more citizen-focused approach to policing. This meant that the major focus of the police was finally switched to dealing with the issues within the community which were of concern to the public at a local level, such as dealing with anti-social behaviour, and raising the confidence of the general public in the whole criminal justice system. This has in turn led to the establishment of locally-based neighbourhood policing teams of police officers, community support officers, special constables and in some areas local authority street wardens.

Since its launch in 2008, each police force across the United Kingdom worked along national guidelines to develop a policing pledge (or alternatively a policing charter or set of values). The policing pledge set out a series of 'promises' that each force made to the community that they police and the services which the force will provide together with those services which the community can expect. For example, the pledge included treating all individuals fairly and with respect and the provision of information to the community on its neighbourhood policing team. In the case of policing pledges, especially there was an aim to answer all emergency calls within ten seconds and for neighbourhood policing teams to spend 80 per cent of their time visibly within the community. In June 2010, the home secretary, Theresa May, announced that the policing pledge was to be scrapped, instead turning the focus of the police to cutting crime and anti-social behaviour (Home Office, 2010c). This transition of the focus of the police once more to fighting crime is bound to leave the police service with a community-focused legacy, and one would hope, with the associated benefits created by the introduction of the policing pledge.

# Case study section

To help you to understand the important part each of the job roles described performs within the modern policing team, a fictional extended case study starts here and will be returned to within each chapter of the book. Self-assessment questions relating to each role are also provided to check your knowledge and understanding.

The case study deals with an armed robbery which has taken place within a busy town centre and details how the police would first respond to the incident, how it would be investigated and how those arrested would be detained prior to appearing in court.

---

## An Introduction

*The ten-hour shift for the neighbourhood policing team due to commence at 2 p.m. started 15 minutes early, with eight police officers and two community support officers being briefed by a police sergeant and an inspector. The team is also expected to be joined by two special constables at 5 p.m., who will each work a four-hour shift.*

*Between them, the neighbourhood policing teams are responsible for policing a busy town centre sub-division which consists of 15,000 residents, together with 9,000 employees and over 12,000 visitors who travel daily into the town. Within the sub-division, there are several square kilometres of houses, apartments, shops, pubs, restaurants, fast food outlets, a sports centre, an industrial unit and a bus station.*

*During the shift briefing, those present were allocated specific duties, such as high-visibility foot patrols in areas of recent crimes and anti-social behaviour. Other individuals were directed to check intelligence reports on the police force intranet in relation to crime types and those suspected of being involved in such crime, and essential information was passed on, including the availability of specific force resources such as the helicopter and dogs section.*

*At 2 p.m. as team members were collecting their airwaves secure mobile communication radio sets, a call came over the radio for the two officers allocated to foot patrol in the town centre to assist response police officers who were attending the report of a robbery taking place in a nearby town centre newsagents. The officers acknowledged their request to attend the scene of the reported robbery and swiftly set off on foot to aid their colleagues.*

---

REFERENCES

Casey, L (2008) *Engaging Communities in Fighting Crime – Executive Summary*. London: Cabinet Office.

Donnelly, D and Scott, K (2008) Policing in Scotland, in Newburn, T (ed) *Handbook of Policing*, 2nd edition. Cullompton: Willan Publishing.

Flanagan, R (2008) *The Review of Policing*. London: Home Office.

HMIC (2011) *Demanding Times: The Front Line and Police Visibility*. London: Her Majesty's Inspectorate of Constabulary.

Home Office (1988) *Civilian Staff in the Police Service, Circular 105/88*. London: Home Office.

Home Office (2010a) *Home Office Statistical Bulletin: Police Service Strength, 31 March 2010, Research*. London: Development and Statistics Directorate.

Home Office (2010b) *Policing in the 21st Century: Reconnecting Police and the People.* London: Home Office. Norwich: TSO.

Home Office (2010c) Theresa May's speech to the National Policing Conference, Tuesday, 29 June 2010. Available online at www.homeoffice.gov.uk/media-centre/speeches/theresa-may-sp-NPC (accessed 22 July 2010).

Leigh, A, Read, T and Tilley, N (1996) *Problem-Oriented Policing: Brit Pop. Crime Detection and Prevention Series Paper 75.* London: Home Office.

Metropolitan Police (2010) *Met Careers in London: Frequently Asked Questions.* Available online at www.met.police.uk/careers/faq.html (accessed 23 March 2011).

Metropolitan Police Authority and Metropolitan Police Service (2009) *Summary of 2009–2012 Policing London Business Plan.* London: Metropolitan Police Authority.

Mulcahy, A (2008) The Police Service of Northern Ireland, in Newburn T (ed) *Handbook of Policing,* 2nd edition. Cullompton: Willan Publishing.

Pepper, I and McGrath, R (2010) Pre-employment Course: A Partnership for Success? *Education and Training,* 52(3): 245–54.

Rowe M (2008) *Introduction to Policing.* London: Sage.

Skills for Justice (2009) *Justice Sector Almanac.* Sheffield: Skills for Justice.

Stinson, V, Patry, M and Smith, S (2007) The CSI Effect: Reflections from Police and Forensic Investigators. *The Canadian Journal of Police and Security Services,* 5(3/4): 125–33.

Winsor, T (2011) *Independent Review of Police Officer and Staff Remuneration and Conditions, Part 1 Report.* London: HMSO.

# 1 Initial report of an incident: the role of the call taker/ control room dispatcher

SAMANTHA SCOTT

---

### CHAPTER OBJECTIVES

By the end of this chapter you will have:

- developed an understanding of the recruitment, training, role and progression of the call taker and control room dispatcher;
- understood the complexities involved in working within a control room.

---

## Introduction

This chapter primarily explores two roles within the emergency control room (CR).

- Call taker.

- CR dispatcher.

Originally these two roles were seen as one, with the automatic expectation that an experienced call taker would eventually move onto the dispatching role once they had demonstrated a high level of service and ability in the call taking arena. In some forces, this is no longer the case, with differing job and person specifications and varying salary scales. Therefore, this chapter looks at both the role of the call taker and the dispatching role in order to highlight differential tasks, with a discussion on how both roles can progress.

## What is a call taker or control room dispatcher?

Since 1937, police forces across the United Kingdom have implemented and utilised the 999 emergency services system (Her Majesty's Inspectorate of Constabulary [HMIC], 2001). The way in which calls have been handled during that period has differed between regions, with some forces utilising force intelligence rooms which only dealt with emergency incidents and managed radio channels (Clarke et al.,

2003), while other forces commandeered the all-encompassing CRs which would also deal with general advice, information and non-emergency calls.

Since its inception, the level of calls received by the CR has increased, with approximately 67 million calls made to the 999 service every year in the United Kingdom, and recent figures quoted at nearly 80 million (HMIC, 2007). The acknowledgement of the need for more effective communication (HMIC, 2002), the requirement for consistency for incident grading and performance indicators and uniformity throughout force CRs (Bain et al., 2005) have all been continually stressed by governmental agencies and the criminal justice system with studies conducted, and White papers and reports subsequently released, to address areas that were falling below acceptable levels.

The implementation of the National Standards for Incident Recording (NSIR) sought to improve the way in which incidents were recorded and dealt with on a national level, with the aim of producing a clearer picture. In 2003 the Police Skills and Standards Organisation noted that approximately 12,000 police staff were employed within the communications centres. The importance of this is highlighted by Bain et al. (2005) who point out that the first contact that a witness or victim has with the police can often be via the telephone.

The initial contact that a member of the public makes to the police is via a police call taker (sometimes called a control room operator), and this is often the first time a member of the public has had any dealings with the police. It has been recognised by the HMIC (2005) that this can be a very unnerving experience for many. The response the caller gets from the person on the other end of the line can not only determine the effectiveness of the outcome of the incident and the quality of the information that is attained but can also shape the perception of the police service as a whole (Skogan, 1996). It is, therefore, imperative that the person chosen for the role has a variety of skills, attributes, appropriate previous experience in a similar role and the ability to portray the air of professionalism at all times, in highly difficult and distressing situations.

# Job description

Below is a generic job description for a call taker. This gives some idea of what the police would look for in a potential employee.

# Job purpose

- To undertake the role of CR call taker, ensuring callers are routed correctly, giving quality help and advice to callers and using innovative ideas to deal with the community's problems.

- To promote equality of opportunity and treat all individuals fairly with dignity and respect.

- To provide a high-quality, customer-focused service, in accordance with the Staff Charter.

# Core work areas

Answer all emergency 999 calls and non-emergency calls within force and national targets, have the ability to operate computerised systems accurately and treat all callers with respect and courtesy while obtaining accurate information promptly.

Create incident logs in line with NSIR and ensure that all information is accurate and complies with national legislation.

Use problem-solving skills and attempt to resolve queries in a professional and timely manner, which is acceptable to both the caller and the force.

When advising a caller, ensure a sufficient level of knowledge to advise the party appropriately. An incident log should be created and updated with all of the information given.

Inform the control inspector, sergeant and supervisor promptly of any serious incidents and any other matter requiring a supervisor's attention, that is, serious road traffic collisions (RTCs), firearms incidents or pursuits.

Understand and enforce corporate policy as regards the use and abuse of the 999 emergency phone system, recording all misuse accordingly.

# Other duties

The post holder will be required to carry out such other duties as may be determined from time to time within the general scope of the post. Duties and responsibilities outside the general scope of the post will only be required with the further consent of the post holder.

# What does the role involve?

A 999 call will come to the CR via a direct emergency line. In some CRs, this will flash up on the computer screens of the call taker to alert them to the call and may be accompanied by an audible signal (Dowling, 2010). It is expected that the call will be answered within ten seconds (Caless, 2010). The majority of calls that come through the emergency CRs tend to be of a non-emergency nature and will be directed to the CR via alternative extension lines. This is due to the fact that the call taker will need to ascertain what the call is about and how it should be graded (Diez, 1995). A call will be graded depending upon the seriousness of the information passed from the caller to the call taker and could vary between a zero priority (which should have come in via the 999 system) and a priority three.

A zero priority would be an emergency situation and would generally mean the call for assistance involves danger to life or property, a violent or serious crime in progress or an RTC with serious injuries (Diez, 1995). It would also be appropriate to assign a zero priority if a suspect is still on scene or if there is a high probability that the suspects will be arrested if police attend the scene rapidly (Houghton et al., 2006). This type of call is sent via computer by the call taker direct to the CR dispatcher who must assign the job to an appropriate police unit within two minutes to hit the required dispatching target. The available unit can be identified via the dispatcher's computer screen, by asking over the radio system for assistance, and in some forces an Automatic Vehicle Location Systems (ALVS) and Automatic Person Location Systems (APLS) will advise the CR of which police unit is closest to the scene (Jane's Police Product Review, 2009, p 4). This process is assisted by the use of effective and more available mobile technologies (Sorensen and Pica, 2005; Mason, 2010) and integrated CRs (Lampard, 2009). The police unit on the ground then have up to eight minutes to attend/arrive at the incident, in order for the response time to equate to a total of ten minutes or less in an urban area, which is increased to 20 minutes in more rural locations. What must be highlighted is that the times given are the maximum, with zero priority calls generally being attended at a much more rapid rate.

*Incident Example – level 0: A call is received from a male who has just been involved in an RTC. The car has plummeted into a deep ditch. The male describes his injuries, and it is rapidly evident that the male is seriously injured and the car is potentially in a position which will make it difficult to gain access to the victim. The male can also see he is badly injured and is becoming weak and incoherent. The call taker needs to keep the injured man talking and alert as much as possible while waiting for the paramedics and informing the ambulance service, the fire brigade and the dispatchers of the location.*

A level 1 incident is where the incident is still of a serious nature, but the perpetrator is no longer on the scene and there is no threat to life (Table 1.1). The current requirement is that incidents graded at level 1 will be dispatched within 30 minutes with the response officers also attending within 30 minutes for attendance to be within one hour of reporting (Dowling, 2010).

A level 2 incident needs to be dealt with within an acceptable time frame for both the police service and the victim (or injured party, also known as the IP), and an estimated time of arrival would be given to the person reporting, but would not exceed 24 hours.

A level 3 incident is where a response time would be agreed with the IP or victim of the crime. The current situation in relation to attendance at a crime is that everything reported receives a visit from a police officer or unit. There are, of course, exceptions with each call evaluated on an individual basis identifying vulnerability or distress levels of the victims and responding accordingly, as well as the actual details of the crime/incident itself (Caless, 2010).

*Table 1.1  Incident level guide*

| Incident levels at a glance | To meet the grade requirements |
| --- | --- |
| Level 0 | Danger to life |
| | Violence used or threatened |
| | Especially vulnerable victim |
| | Suspect of a serious crime in the immediate vicinity |
| | Serious crime in progress |
| | RTC involving serious personal injury |
| | Give target arrival time |
| Level 1 | Serious incident but no perpetrator on scene and no threat to life |
| | Give target arrival time |
| Level 2 | Crime has occurred but does not fit level 0 or level 1 criteria; attendance must be within 24 hours. Estimated time of arrival to be given to the victim |
| Level 3 | Minor crime or complaint. Estimated time of arrival to be agreed with the victim or complainant |

# Recruitment into the role

Initially, recruitment into the role of call taker is advertised within the local media, within force orders and internally throughout the service. You cannot become a dispatcher without first working as a call taker within the police service. This is owing to the fact that the candidate needs to gain experience and demonstrate numerous abilities and qualities prior to moving into the dispatcher's chair. The role of the call taker and the dispatcher is very complex. The ability to multi-task, utilise highly technical equipment and manage your well-being in a very high-stress environment while still delivering accurate, timely and quality service to the general public and your police colleagues does not suit all and cannot be achieved by just anyone. The person specification is separated into a number of areas, which are stated as desirable qualities or essential qualities. A desirable quality would be closely-related experience or working within the public sector, with the ability to communicate with people from diverse backgrounds. An essential quality relates to skills or qualities that can be proven. These may include:

- good verbal, communication and problem-solving skills;
- good attendance within previous employment roles;
- an ability to work autonomously when required;
- an ability to confidently use numerous computerised packages.

The candidate can be assessed in a number of ways for the role. These may include the completion of an application form and supporting statement giving reasons for wanting to work within policing, psychometric testing after shortlisting and/or through more in-depth probing during the interview process.

> *Incident Example – level 0: A very early morning call is received, in which the call taker can hear the whisper of a female. As the woman is talking she begins to cry which makes it difficult for the call taker to understand what is being said. The female cannot raise her voice, as she has become aware of intruders downstairs in her home. The female is home alone, and if she raises her voice, it could potentially put her at risk and alert the intruders to her whereabouts. It is imperative that the female is kept on the phone until the police arrive. It is the job of the call taker to keep the female as calm as possible and to obtain as much information as is possible, regarding her location and that of the intruders to assist the officers responding.*

## Qualifications

A call taker is expected to have a minimum of either NVQ Level 3 or equivalent in a customer care role or substantial experience in a customer service environment. Good levels of written English are also of high importance due to the exacting nature of the role, as is the ability to type at speed, since printed copies of typed computer entries may be used as evidence in legal proceedings.

## Skills and qualities

In all forces, experience of dealing with vulnerable, angry, frustrated and emotional people or customers is a desirable quality for the call taker. This role is front-line policing. It is very likely that the call taker is the first person within the police service that the caller has ever spoken to. The ability to process incoming information and enquiries sensitively and accurately while adapting the communication style to meet each caller is imperative. In police training, there are a number of communication models and methodologies utilised in order for police officers and police staff to deal with the general public. Betaris' Box is one particular model which is widely used for those dealing with emotional or aggressive members of the public. This model illustrates how the way we behave can have an effect on the behaviour and the attitude of the person we are dealing with. If the call taker speaks to a caller negatively, it will be reflected in their voice and will be subconsciously conveyed to the caller. Attitude can come across in voice tone and in certain words which can escalate negative feelings and create conflict between the caller and the call taker.

The Betaris' Box model demonstrates the way attitude can affect behaviour and behaviour can affect attitude (National Police Improvement Agency [NPIA], 2009).

A staff member within a CR must recognise prejudices or bias they have in order to ensure they do not bring them into the role. People react on the phone to the manner in which the person on the other end responds to them. It is the call taker and dispatcher's responsibility to treat everyone fairly and with respect and to react to callers with professionalism under the most difficult of circumstances.

---

*Incident Example – levels 0 and 1: connected incident. The call taker receives a 999 call to alert the police to an RTC. There are two female fatalities. Descriptions and details of the deceased and their cars are passed to the traffic operator by the road traffic officer on the scene. This incident would be graded as a zero priority, and units would be sent within the required time guidelines. The ambulance and fire brigade would also be informed by the call taker and CR and district supervision advised.*

*A second 999 call comes in, and this time it's from a very concerned elderly gentleman whose wife hasn't returned home. Upon obtaining details and information from the caller, it becomes obvious that one of the females killed in the road traffic accident is the wife of the caller. The experienced operator needs to keep the caller talking on line while informing their supervisor of the incident in order for a response unit to be sent to the home of the caller. The call taker cannot give information of a death over the phone or make the caller aware of the circumstances. The call taker needs to remain calm and talk on the phone until the police officer arrives to handle the situation in person. This incident would not be graded as a zero; it would be graded at level 1, however; due to the nature of the call, units would be sent to attend as a matter of urgency.*

---

# Call taker training

The training for a call taker and a dispatcher can vary slightly from force area to force area. However, the training method described below is still the current policy in a North East force and can be used for illustrative purposes.

Before a police staff uniform is issued, a call taker must first undertake a probationary period of approximately six months. Within this time, various types of training are provided to prepare the call taker for their future role. For the first two weeks, call training is given on a mock-up call station. This allows the new recruit to experience the differing style of calls that can be expected, from the calm victim of a burglary, to the injured victim of a physical attack, to the hysterical caller, the irate caller and also the confused caller who is not aware of their surroundings. This gives the new call taker experience in differing question styles and prepares them for the more emotional and aggressive calls they may receive. The call taker is also given some legal training in order to understand what a crime is and the different categories that crimes fall into. Talks are given by other units within the force, for example, the drugs team and the domestic violence team, to prepare the person for a number of scenarios.

After the initial two weeks of training, the new call taker is assigned to a tutor, who sits with them on a dual-control console for four weeks. This allows the new employee to learn, by example, how to deal with calls in a live situation. Once the call taker is confident of taking the calls, the tutor continually assesses the call and can interject at any time should the need arise. At the six-week point, the tutor then moves to the adjacent console, to be close at hand but allowing the call taker to work alone.

Some forces have now implemented formal training courses for their call takers, to train them in the ways of investigation. This includes understanding the difference between open and closed questioning, problem solving, acquiring good local knowledge and gaining an awareness of neighbourhood policing teams (NPTs) in order to assist callers more quickly, while obtaining the optimum amount of information to assist the police and force intelligence (Jane's Police Review, 2010).

During the probationary period, the call taker spends a number of shifts with the traffic department, crime scene investigation department, dog section, air support and the response units. This gives the call taker experience of what it is like on the streets for the police officer and provides first-hand knowledge of the difficulties that the officers face. At the six-month stage, a review of performance is undertaken by CR supervision along with the tutor. At this point, the probation period is complete and the call taker is given a uniform and deemed to be trained.

Intensive training is important in relation to call taking, as it has been found that incorrect call handling or lack of training with particular types of call can result in the loss of life. Call takers with limited training in mapping systems or a lack of understanding of risk from threatening callers have previously been noted by the Independent Police Complaints Commission as contributing to the deaths of members of the general public (Pertile, 2010; Jane's Police Review, 2010). It is, therefore, imperative that training is intensive and thorough and also that the operator is continually assessed throughout their career.

> *Incident Example – level 2: A theft has occurred in a commercial residence while the owner was dealing with another customer. A box full of mobile phones has been taken, and the caller is irate. There are no witnesses to the incident, and no CCTV is available. The caller demands immediate attendance, however; although the incident is serious for the owner, it does not fulfil level 0 or level 1 criteria and would therefore be assigned as a level 2 attendance.*

# Dispatcher training

The role of the dispatcher differs from that of the call taker due to the fact that the dispatcher deals directly with the police units on patrol via radio and does not take the initial incoming emergency calls. They do still, however, have contact with the public, if there is a requirement to obtain more details regarding an incident.

To become a dispatcher, the call taker needs to have a good level of experience and show ability to deal with highly stressful situations. The original tutor the call taker was given at the commencement of their post is assigned to them again on the dispatcher station. The trainee dispatcher remains with the tutor for four weeks, working a particular area of the force. Once confident with all the computer systems and procedures, the tutor then sits on the adjacent control, prior to the dispatcher being allowed to go solo.

# Potential for role and career progression

Within the CR, there are a number of roles that the experienced staff member can move into. From call taker to dispatcher, you can go on to be a traffic operator, a major incident operator, an integrated records information system (IRIS) operator, a dedicated instant closure officer (DICO) and a CR tutor.

## Traffic operator

The traffic operator is also known as an LZ operator. These staff members are usually very experienced dispatchers who deal only with the traffic section. A strong geographical knowledge and directional sense is required, as LZ also deals with enquiries from police officers and the general public who need to be given location knowledge and advice.

## Major incident operator

The major incident operator works within the major incident room. This role oversees the running of all the communications and incident logging and liaising with control and district supervision, as well as all police units on the ground and in the air (Lindberg, 2010). A major incident could be anything from a serious chemical spillage and tanker overturning to a major RTC, to a child/person abduction or the discovery of a body. It allows a continual flow of dialogue and detailed recording of the step-by-step processes involved in dealing with and investigating a serious incident.

## Dedicated instant closure officer

A DICO is an experienced CR operator who only deals with the closure of jobs once the incidents have been dealt with by a police unit. It is the DICO's responsibility to speak directly to the public, and in particular to the person who reported a crime, to assess how the police dealt with the situation and advise on the next steps. Only when both the police and the IP are satisfied with the outcome of the response to an incident will the job be officially recorded as closed.

## Integrated records information system operator

An IRIS operator is responsible for updating the intelligence system, once referred to as the Central Intelligence System. All potentially important information gathered by CR or police officers dealing with an incident, or from general observations, is logged on the IRIS:

> *Fundamentally, the system records details of people, organisations (including criminal organisations), businesses, property, locations, events, associations, vehicles and the sophisticated relationship between them. The force is committed to delivering the four data inputs interfaces into IRIS, these are custody – arrest/key event intelligence report, street encounters, crime and video witness.*

(Cleveland Police, 2010)

The dedicated operator is responsible for continually updating this intelligence information, for when it is required.

## Control room supervisor

There is also the management route to become CR supervisor. This role oversees all staffing and rotas to ensure that the correct amount of staff are on call taker and the dispatching and LZ stations to provide optimum service to the public. As the role is managing staff members, there is also the personal and pastoral care of the staff, and any complaints and discipline issues also need to be addressed. A number of CR staff also go on to apply for the role of a police officer once they have gained experience within the force.

---

*Incident Example – level 3: A call is received at 10 a.m. in the morning from a member of Neighbourhood Watch. He has been advised that local residents are complaining of large groups of youths congregating around the youth club after 9 p.m. on an evening. Although the youngsters have not caused any damage, the noise they create is disturbing the neighbours who live in close proximity to the club. The caller wants to speak to an officer about the situation to see if any measures can be taken to resolve the situation. This incident would be graded at level 3, and the NPTs or local beat officers would be advised of the situation. A time would be agreed with the complainant to arrange a meeting with a police officer to discuss the problem.*

---

**C H A P T E R   S U M M A R Y**

The roles of the call taker and the emergency CR dispatcher were explored as front-line policing positions. It is the CR staff who are often the first point of contact, with the general public in both emergencies and non-emergency situations. Staff are highly trained and are able to deal with a magnitude of stressful and challenging occurrences on a daily basis. The importance of these roles was explored as an important part of the team within the wider policing family.

---

CASE STUDY

*Now that you fully understand the role of the CR operator you can see how it works in practice, as our case study continues …*

*At 2 p.m. as each team member was collecting their airwaves secure mobile communication radio set, a call came over the radio for the two officers allocated to foot patrol in the town centre to assist response police officers who were attending the report of a robbery taking place in a nearby town centre newsagents. The officers acknowledged their request to attend the scene of the reported robbery and swiftly set off on foot to aid their colleagues.*

*At 1.58 p.m., a call is received in CR. The computer is flashing, and an audible sound can be heard, alerting the call taker to the fact that the call is an emergency.*

*'Hello, Police Emergency …'*

*The British Telecom (BT) operator advises the call taker that the number comes from an address in the town centre and passes on the phone number. The BT operator takes this information in case the call is terminated for any reason, so the Police can then locate the location of the caller if necessary. The caller comes onto the line …*

*Victim: 'We've been robbed, you need to get someone here now … we're the newsagents on the High Street … he's taken the money, he's taken the money!'*

*The address is quickly inputted into the computer, and the Intergraph mapping system finds the location. The call taker assigns the job type and sends it to the dispatcher as a zero priority.*

*Call taker: 'Officers are en route madam, can you tell me what your name is? … Are the suspects still on the premises? … Is anyone hurt? … Can you give me any description of the intruders? … Were they on foot or in a vehicle? … Are the suspects still in view? … Did you see which direction they went? … Is anyone else in the shop with you, another staff member, a member of the public? … Did anyone else witness the incident? …'*

*Responses to the questions are typed into the computer, allowing the dispatcher to update the response officers and also supervision, as well as continuing a running commentary over the airwaves.*

*Dispatcher: 'We have a zero priority …. a robbery in Roman's Newsagents in the High Street, availability for attendance?'*

*Police van: 'M171, please show us attending'.*

*Dispatcher: 'M171, received'.*

---

*The dispatcher assigns the job in the queue to the unit which has declared its availability. While en route the response team is updated with all of the information received from the call taker, including incident details, description(s) of the suspect(s), direction of travel, any injuries and the names of the people they are going to meet at the premises.*

*Dispatcher: 'M1 to all units, observations for two males involved in a robbery at Roman's Newsagents in the High Street. The first male is described as 5 foot 10 inches tall, wearing a red and white striped football top, and black tracksuit bottoms and black tracksuit jacket. Male is IC1 with black spiked hair. The second suspect is approximately 5 foot tall, IC3 with a shaven head, wearing a blue t-shirt, white tracksuit top and blue jeans. They have headed on foot towards the town centre mall'.*

*The dispatcher monitors the computerised mapping system of where the incident has taken place and advises M171 on the quickest route to the scene.*

*Police van: 'M171 to M1, please show us as arriving'.*

*Dispatcher: 'M171 received'.*

*The unit notices a crowd gathering and requests backup from the town centre NPT in order to assist. The local foot beat have just come on duty, so the dispatcher requests backup via the radio.*

*Foot patrol: 'M1, please show the NPT as en route to the scene'.*

*Dispatcher: 'M1 to NPT, message received and understood'.*

*Police van: 'M171 to M1, further information from the victims lead us to believe that there may be a firearm involved in the robbery, which the original caller was not aware of. Another staff member of the shop states that they believe one of the suspects may have had a weapon hidden under his jacket but could not be completely sure. Nobody actually saw the weapon, but the suspect made gestures underneath his coat that led this staff member to believe that one of the suspects was carrying a firearm. A witness has also advised us that he believes the suspects ran to a car, a red Ford Focus, with a partial registration TU10 X\*\*'.*

*Dispatcher: 'Roger M171, information received, performing the checks now'.*

*The dispatcher immediately performs a partial vehicle check on the Police National Computer (PNC) which narrows the identity of the car down to one possibility.*

*'M1 to M171, PNC shows that the car was stolen at 4 a.m., earlier today. M1 to all units, observation for a red Ford Focus TU10 XXX. The passengers are believed to have been involved in a robbery at Roman's Newsagents in the High Street. Please do not approach the vehicle, as the armed response unit is being assigned to the location, but inform dispatch or LZ immediately regarding any sightings'.*

*Owing to the information regarding the possible firearm, this incident now becomes a serious concern for the public and therefore the CR supervisor takes over from the dispatcher as the incident commander (Arbuthnot, 2008). At this point, the dispatcher contacts the air support unit helicopter to request assistance to cover the densely populated area by using their helicopter camera to stream live pictures back to CR via an IT downlink. The incident commander (the CR inspector) informs the district inspector of the developing details of the incident and the change of command. The armed response vehicle is assigned to the incident by the commander ...*

# Self-assessment questions

1. In which year was the 999 Emergency Services number implemented?

2. What is the difference between a force intelligence room and a CR?

3. Why were NSIR implemented?

4. How rapidly should a 999 call be answered?

5. When would an incident be graded as a zero priority by a call taker?

6. What do the acronyms ALVS and APLS stand for?

7. What is the required dispatch and arrival time for a priority 1 incident?

8. How can IRIS assist the dispatcher?

9. What communication model describes how attitude can affect behaviour?

10. Who would take the role of incident commander in a firearms incident?

*FURTHER READING*

Bain, P, Taylor, P and Dutton, E (2005) *The Thin Front Line: Call Handling in Police Control Rooms*. 23rd International Labour Process Conference. Glasgow.

Her Majesty' s Inspectorate of Constabulary (HMIC) (2007) *Beyond the Call – A Thematic Inspection of Police Contact Centres' Contribution to Incident Management*. London: The Stationery Office.

Police Skills and Standards Organisation (PSSO) (2003) *Public Sector: A Thematic Skills Foresight Report on Communications and Call Handling*. London: The Stationery Office.

*REFERENCES*

Arbuthnot, K (2008) A Command Gap? A Practitioner's Analysis of the Value of Comparisons Between the UK's Military and Emergency Service's Command and Control Models in the Context of UK Resilience Operations. *Journal of Contingencies and Crisis Management,* 16(4): 186–95.

Bain, P, Taylor, P and Dutton, E (2005) *The Thin Front Line: Call Handling in Police Control Rooms*. 23rd International Labour Process Conference. Glasgow.

Caless, B (2010) *PCSO Handbook*, 2nd edition. Oxford: Oxford University Press.

Clarke, S, Lehaney, B and Evans, H (2003) A Study of a UK Police Call Centre, in Khosrow-Pour M (ed) *Information Technology and Organisations: Trends, Issues, Challenges and Solutions*, volume 1. London: Ideal Group.

Cleveland Police (2010) *Corporate Planning and Performance Unit.* Available online at www.cleveland.police.uk/about-us/Glossary.aspx (accessed 16 July 2010).

Diez, L (1995) *The Use of Call Grading: How Calls to the Police Are Graded and Resourced.* Police Research Series Paper Number 13. London: Home Office Police Department.

Dowling, A (2010) Conversation with Alison Dowling, Police HQ, Control Room (17 May 2010).

Her Majesty' s Inspectorate of Constabulary (HMIC) (2001) *Open All Hours – A Thematic Inspection of the Role of Police Visibility & Accessibility in Public Reassurance.* London: HMIC.

Her Majesty' s Inspectorate of Constabulary (HMIC) (2002) *Justice for All.* London: The Stationery Office.

Her Majesty' s Inspectorate of Constabulary (HMIC) (2005) *First Contact – A Thematic Inspection of Police Contact Management.* London: The Stationery Office.

Her Majesty' s Inspectorate of Constabulary (HMIC) (2007) *Beyond the Call – A Thematic Inspection of Police Contact Centres' Contribution to Incident Management.* London: The Stationery Office.

Houghton, R, Baber, C, McMaster, R, Stanton, N, A, Salmon, P, Stewart, R and Walker, G (2006) Command and Control in Emergency Services Operation: A Social Network Analysis. *Ergonomics*, 49(12): 1204–25.

Jane's Police Product Review (2009) Electronic Tagging … For Officers: UK Force is Trialling System to Keep Closer Track of Vehicle and Personnel. *Jane's Police Product Review*, 32: 4.

Jane's Police Review (2010) Force Trains Staff in New Phone Manner. *Jane's Police Review*, 118(6066): 5.

Lampard, S (2009) Integrate to Accumulate. *Jane's Police Product Review*, 30: 34–5.

Lindberg, E Cleveland Police, Control Room . 17 May 2010. Personal Communication.

Mason, G. (2010) Wireless Coppers. *Jane's Police Review*, 118(6064): 24–5.

National Police Improvement Agency (NPIA) (2009) *IPLDP Quick Notes.* Version 1.09. London: The Stationery Office.

Pertile, E (2010) Call-handling Errors Cost Lives, Warn IPCC. *Jane's Police Review*, 118(6068): 8.

Police Skills and Standards Organisation (PSSO) (2003) *Public Sector: A Thematic Skills Foresight Report on Communications and Call Handling.* London: The Stationery Office.

Skogan, W G (1996) The Police and Public Opinion in Britain. *American Behavioural Scientist*, 39(4): 421–32.

Sorensen, C and Pica D (2005) Tales from the Police: Rhythms of Interaction with Mobile Technologies. *Information and Organisation*, 15: 125–9.

# 2 First police response: police officers, special constables and community support officers

CHRIS BLAKE

### CHAPTER OBJECTIVES

By the end of this chapter you will have:

- developed knowledge and understanding of the recruitment, training and roles of police officers, special constables and community support officers;
- understood the key skills and qualities required of these roles.

## Introduction

This chapter primarily explores a brief history and the functions of the three roles within operational front-line policing.

- Police officer.

- Special constable.

- Community support officer.

## Front-line policing in context

The police have been depicted as underpinning modern civilisation and democracy and as being responsible for *bringing security without which civilisation is impossible* (Critchley, 1978, p 321).

The origins of policing stem from early tribal history with law and order emanating through the laws and customs of the Danes and Anglo-Saxons. Methods of maintaining public order changed considerably after Norman feudalism, and the nearest equivalent to modern policing seems to be the Anglo-Saxon 'tything' system where people were grouped into a 'tything' of ten people with a tything man representing each group. In effect, the people were the police, and this became widely established in the seventeenth and eighteenth centuries with one unarmed citizen being appointed or elected annually to serve as parish constable for a year and to secure observance of laws and maintaining order.

The eighteenth century witnessed migrations between towns and cities brought about by vast social and economic changes, as well as the failure of the parish constable and 'Watch' systems. Early nineteenth-century criminal justice and punishment was seen as *very severe ... with weak and capricious enforcement machinery* (Philips, 1983, p 54). This led to the formation of the 'New Police' in 1829. The 1856 County and Borough Police Act later established the Her Majesty's Inspectorate of Constabulary (HMIC) and a better balance between the responsibilities of the local government, the justices and the central government. Other acts aimed at improving policing within England and Wales include the Police Acts of 1964, 2004 and 2006, although this is not an exhaustive list.

Policing has been characterised as a public service with a doctrine of independence, insulated from central and local government control and as an autonomous servant of the law. But the role of the central government in determining local priorities and performance has grown resulting in a 'disconnection' between the police and the public. This has been linked to bureaucracy and the government's preoccupation with micro-management and target setting (Home Office, 2010a). Therefore, the Police Reform and Social Responsibility Bill aims to restore this 'connection' by reducing targets and giving the public a direct say on how neighbourhoods should be policed.

> This [is] ... the most radical change to policing in 50 years. We will transfer power in policing – replacing bureaucratic accountability with democratic accountability.
>
> (Home Office, 2010a, p 5)

The Bill aims to replace police authorities with directly elected police and crime commissioners with a single commissioner elected for each force in England, with the exception of the:

- Metropolitan Police and City of London Police;

- British Transport Police;

- Civil Nuclear Constabulary;

- Ministry of Defence Police.

In London the Metropolitan Police Authority will be abolished and the Greater London Authority will fulfil a scrutiny role.

Commissioners will be accountable for the performance of their respective police services and expected to work with their local communities in establishing local crime and anti-social behaviour (ASB) priorities through a strategic plan. Furthermore, the government plans to cut unnecessary bureaucracy by removing any remaining police targets, in particular the 'Policing Pledge' which has been described as *ten targets in disguise* (Home Office, 2010a, para 3.5).

# Patrol officer: qualifications and recruitment into the role

Entry to the police service is open to almost everyone provided selection procedures are met, including fitness and medical standards. This is followed by a two-year training programme – the Initial Police Learning and Development Programme (IPLDP) – which involves classroom and work-based learning. Training and development then continues throughout a police officer's career with opportunities for further progression within the service.

Although there isn't a formal educational requirement for entry to the police service, key skills are needed to enable an individual to effectively manage the challenges in policing. Some are critical in the prevention and detection of crime and in the apprehension of offenders, the overwhelming majority of whom tend to suffer from mental difficulties or from substance misuse (Wright and Waddington, 2010). Police officers need to be calm, resilient and diplomatic. They need to act with integrity and be able to communicate effectively. Moreover, investigating crime and dealing with significant amounts of paperwork also calls for good standards of literacy.

Because these skills were loosely defined, assessment methods tended to vary across the regions. Now, Skills for Justice (SFJ) is responsible for ensuring that those working within the justice sector have the appropriate skills to do their job. Structured activities listed within a competency framework provide role definition and guidance on recruitment, registers of competence, promotion and career progression. The Integrated Competency Framework (ICF) lists and describes the attributes, attitudes and behaviours necessary to become a police officer, and applicants are tested through a variety of exercises, some interactive, some written, including numerical and verbal reasoning tests (Skills for Justice, 2009).

It should be noted that a new Policing Professional Framework (PPF) will be rolled out during 2011 and the suite of exercises currently used are due to be replaced by 2012. Pre-eminent within the PPF, the National Occupational Standards will instead be used to describe and explain the various activities that police and support staff now perform. Behavioural requirements will also sit within the framework.

Assessment is currently based on seven behaviours taken from the SFJ (ICF, 2009 version 10).

1. Effective communication.
2. Team working.
3. Problem solving.
4. Community and customer focus.
5. Respect for race and diversity.
6. Personal responsibility.
7. Resilience.

# Key skills and qualities

## Effective communication

This key skill ranks at or near the top of the list of essential policing qualities. Police officers need to speak with authority and confidence and be able to communicate their needs and intentions clearly; they need to alter their style of communication to suit a particular audience; they need to listen actively to what others are saying while taking time to understand the points being made. It is important, too, that they ask appropriate questions without interrupting at inappropriate times. Finally, they need to produce well-structured written reports and summaries with supporting arguments and effective recommendations.

## Team working

Belbin defines and explains team working as ... *behaving, contributing and inter-relating with others in a particular way* ... (2010, p 35). This includes understanding specific roles and responsibilities so that individual contributions can be enhanced. Tuckman's (1965) well-coined phrase, *forming, storming, norming and performing*, is used to describe the path to effective team working which is an essential, but sometimes difficult, skill. The team member needs to be approachable and friendly, willing to provide and ask for and accept assistance, be willing to accept unpopular or routine tasks and actively support the team to reach its objectives.

## Problem solving

Since Goldstein (1990) first introduced the problem-solving approach to policing there has been a significant increase in 'demand'-led policing, marking a significant change to the actual nature of policing. To be more effective when responding to crime, nuisance and disorder, the police and other agencies have adopted two separate, though interrelated, strategies. Community-oriented policing and problem-oriented or problem-solving policing are proactive problem-solving strategies, and as one analysis notes:

> ... *providing service to the community is the very nature of police work* ...
>
> (Peak and Glensor, 1996, p 179)

It is generally agreed that problem solving is a key component to effective community policing with its focus on analysing specific elements of the problem. Therefore, appropriate emphasis is given to the systematic identification of relevant and important issues and events. Any information needs to be promptly collated and retrieved so that logical conclusions can be drawn and correct decisions made. Moreover, a police officer needs to be impartial at all times and must refrain from drawing inappropriate conclusions.

## Community and customer focus

'Customer or citizen focus' is a term often used when referring to the needs and priorities of people, particularly when designing and implementing policing services. Stimulated by the apparent decline in levels of public trust and confidence in the police, attempts have been made to reconfigure the delivery of policing so that it is 'citizen focused' and more effective in responding to local concerns. This has been driven by the notion of a 'reassurance gap', where, despite the overall reduction in levels of crime during the last decade, there is a perception that crime is increasing.

In 2009 the government introduced a single confidence target jointly for police and local authorities which required a sustained commitment to enhance satisfaction and confidence in policing. Research shows that the police have not fared particularly well when it comes to developing public confidence, unlike other public sector services where satisfaction tends to increase with contact (Blaug et al., 2006). In 2008, HMIC identified areas for improvement in every force (HMIC, 2008), and similar research by Consumer Focus (2010) and HMIC (2009) indicates that almost a third of the people who had come into contact with the police were unhappy with the quality of service, or the response they had received. Difficulties in contacting the police, the unhelpful attitude of some officers and the view that their concerns had been trivialised were among the key reasons for dissatisfaction. Recent research into consumer satisfaction with the public service shows that the police rank low, at 17 out of 23 sectors (Consumer focus, 2010).

It is critical that the police understand what the public wants and the impact of the service it both provides and fails to provide. It is also important that officers present an appropriate image to the public and other organisations. In particular, they should:

- focus on the customer in every activity;
- respond to and resolve customers' problems as quickly as possible;
- apologise when at fault or have made mistakes;
- quickly resolve those errors or mistakes;
- ensure that customers are satisfied with the service they receive;
- manage customer expectations;
- keep customers updated on progress;
- balance community and organisational interests.

## Respect for race and diversity

The enquiry by Sir William Macpherson into the murder of Stephen Lawrence acted as a spur for a series of reports and reforms which promised a fundamental shift in attitudes and police practice. Under the Stephen Lawrence Enquiry Action Plan, community- and race-relations training has been delivered across every police service in England and Wales. The 2005 Police Race and Diversity Learning and Development Programme is now linked to the IPLDP and the wider police reform programme. Central to this is the philosophy that treating people with decency and respect is the most effective way to conduct policing. And following more than four years of reviews, discussions and consultations, the Equalities Act, 2010, consolidates and clarifies discrimination legislation concerning sex, race, disability, sexual orientation, religion or belief and age. It requires that organisations promote equality and avoid discrimination in the workplace.

Although the police service has a collective duty to respect human rights, prevent discrimination and promote equality, individuals representing the organisation are personally responsible for their conduct and need to exhibit the following key skills and qualities:

- Sensitivity when dealing with people's problems and vulnerabilities.

- The ability to recognise issues from different perspectives when resolving disagreements.

- Tolerance and patience when dealing with people both inside and outside the organisation.

- The ability to listen to and value the opinion of others.

- An awareness of the effect that language can have on others.

- The ability to acknowledge and respect different social and cultural customs, beliefs and values.

- A willingness to challenge inappropriate, abusive, aggressive or discriminatory language and/or behaviour.

- A willingness to support minority groups both inside and outside their organisation.

## Personal responsibility

Larry Sherman once remarked that policing *ain't rocket science – it's more difficult*, and research repeatedly demonstrates that the police are called on to deal with an array of matters apart from the usual suspects, crime, nuisance and disorder, for example, being asked to deal with:

- the mentally ill;

- drunken and injured persons;

- missing, elderly and other vulnerable persons;

- sudden and unexpected deaths;

- road hazards and road diversions;

- animal incidents;

- automatic alarms;

- industrial strike action and marchers;

- neighbourhood meetings.

A fundamental principle in any democracy is that the police are accountable for their actions which include both what they do and how they do it. At an individual level, accountability involves conduct with respect to the lawful, courteous and equal treatment of citizens. This is crucial in maintaining the public's trust and confidence if the police are to maintain their legitimacy. This is particularly so in the United Kingdom where policing is undertaken by 43 separate forces on a geographic and not a unitary or national basis.

There is an important link here between police accountability, police discretion and personal responsibility. If we work on the premise that police accountability is having to answer for the exercise of police actions or inactions, then we might reasonably infer that the police have a choice in the exercise of those powers. The appropriate use of 'police discretion' means that individuals who are drawn into the criminal justice system will usually have a case to answer. But regrettably, when discretion is used maliciously or inappropriately, this can damage a community thereby undermining trust and confidence in the police.

Police officers have great discretion whenever the effective limits on their powers enable them to make a choice among possible courses of action or inaction. But having a choice is inherently problematic too. To some degree or another, we are each grounded by culture which is bound by a unique set of social experiences and when, for example, a suspect is arrested, one might suppose that, in violating the officer's 'norms', the suspect has adhered to norms of their own. In this context, the violation of law implies a form of culture conflict, the outcomes of which can be illogical, irrational and irresponsible, for example, the police having to return to an incident which the first officer attending had considered to be 'petty' and had thus ignored or neglected to deal with both the incident and the underlying problems. Professional police officers need to consider and understand the importance of personal responsibility, otherwise they are likely to be called on to deal with the avoidable problems of personal irresponsibility. At this point, you might wish to remind yourself of what Sherman said about policing.

Thus, in practice, personal responsibility actually means:

- taking responsibility for making things happen and achieving results;

- displaying motivation, commitment and perseverance;

- accepting responsibility for personal decisions and actions;

- displaying initiative by taking on tasks and resolving problems;

- taking pride in, and being conscientious in the completion of work;

- following things through to a satisfactory conclusion;

- focusing on a task even when routine;

- improving one's own professional knowledge and keeping it up to date;

- being open, honest and genuine and standing up for what is right;

- making decisions based upon ethical considerations and organisational integrity.

## Resilience

Police officers can witness harrowing scenes and sometimes face situations that a member of the public would find impossible to manage. Incidents like suicides and officer-involved shootings can be life-changing events. But police officers train for these critical incidents and learn to adapt their coping strategies. But when the unexpected happens, one essential factor that will likely determine the outcome is the officer's resilience.

## Consider the following occurrence

A police pursuit ends when the driver of a stolen vehicle loses control and collides with a tree and a child pedestrian. Other persons stand nearby watching anxiously. The child who is unconscious is being attended to by the concerned parent. A semi-conscious passenger has been catapulted through the windscreen and is bleeding profusely from head and face wounds. The driver has run from the scene, and so the officer, who is unaccompanied, decides to first treat the bleeding passenger after calling for an ambulance and further assistance. The officer bandages the wounds before moving to the child whose breathing is shallow. There are no visible injuries, but despite being placed in the recovery position, the child dies at the scene before assistance arrives. The mother becomes distraught and screams at the officer accusing them of neglect and complacency.

What impact do you think the incident will have on the future well-being of the patrol officer? Are they likely to emerge consumed with guilt, anger, doubt, anxiety and perhaps even depression? Or will the officer emerge emotionally stronger and better equipped for the next time? This will depend on a number of factors, such as the availability of psychological support, the media interest and the officer's past training and temperament. It is also clear that recovery, both mentally and physically, will be characterised by a combination of different personal strengths, which include being able to:

- respond calmly, confidently, rationally, logically and decisively in difficult situations;

- make difficult decisions and then have the confidence to see them through before moving on;

- focus, think clearly and remain calm in a difficult situation;

- maintain professional ethics when resolving conflict, hostility and provocation;

- avoid inappropriate emotion and respond to challenges rationally;

- cope with ambiguity and deal with uncertainty and frustration;
- resist pressure to make quick decisions where full consideration is needed;
- stand firmly by a position when it is right to do so.

# What does the role involve?

Although the last decade has seen a marked reduction in overall recorded crime, this needs to be seen in the context of a significant and sustained increase in crime over several decades. And we know from bodies of research that this has contributed to a so-called fear or worry of crime (Mayhew and Hough, 1988). We also understand how media representations of crime can distort the reality, not least by exaggerating the risks and creating a moral panic (Cohen, 2002). This can cause a negative reaction to certain forms of behaviour which reinforces, rather than undermines, the activities concerned. Criminologists have come to refer to this as a 'deviancy amplification spiral' which is perceived to challenge important social values. People become worried about 'deviancy', more fearful of the risk of victimisation and demand a response from the police which can require a sustained effort to bring about appropriate reassurances.

The initial police response to any call from the public ultimately depends on the urgency of the request, which we know from the previous chapter is categorised by the degree of risk and danger. Although we do not question the need for an immediate response to life-threatening incidents, the response to more routine incident(s) can vary according to the incident type, the vulnerability and/or the distress levels involved. The actual response, however, is usually shaped by the availability of deployable resources and so we need to consider, here, the notion of 'greater public involvement' in policing, for example, by having a reserve army of volunteers prepared to act as community crime fighters, similar to fire reservists who help staff some neighbourhood fire stations (Home Office, 2010b, para 5.2).

## Consider the following scenario

The police respond to several reports of youths congregating near a home for elderly persons. The warden at the home is concerned that the presence of the youths is having an unsettling effect on the residents. The youths are acting lawfully and so they are dispersed, only to return the following day.

Discuss this case with your colleagues and consider why the police might have adopted this course of action. How might this be perceived by the youths, the warden, the residents and the local community? What might they do differently the next time and why?

If you are confused about what the police should do, then you might want to consider the Statement of Common (police) Purpose which describes the police role and purpose. It also reminds us of how the police service fundamentally contributes to the democratic maintenance of law and order.

*...the purpose of the police service is to uphold the law fairly and firmly; to prevent crime; to pursue and bring to justice those who break the law; to keep the Queen's peace; to protect, help and reassure the community; and to be seen to do this with integrity, common sense and sound judgement ...*

(Association of Chief Police Officers, 1994, p 87)

The ICF goes further by defining the core responsibilities and activities of a patrol officer, some of which are listed in Table 2.1 overleaf.

# Police officer training

Except for sporadic alterations to the residential elements, the structure and delivery of police training remained unchanged for decades. It was dominated by the need to learn powers and procedures by rote, and through 'job shadowing'. But in the late 1980s, police training became the focus of intense scrutiny and critical comment, with police commentary and debate often being played out under the spotlight of the critical media, particularly television. Although this prompted piecemeal efforts to improve the quality of training, it seems that the real catalyst for change was the HMIC report, Training Matters (Home Office, 2002). It was, therefore, something of a radical change which saw the introduction of the IPLDP in April 2005 (IPLDP Central Authority, 2004) which allowed training to be tailored to meet the local requirements of each police service.

A thematic inspection on workforce modernisation (HMIC, 2004) was seen to focus on the integration and professionalisation of the police service, suggesting multiple points of entry into the service to attract high-quality graduates. Such radical ideas have never been adopted, but it is clear that the modernisation agenda has opened up very real opportunities for a step change and a more integrated approach to police officer training, particularly with joint training as the means of developing standards and off-setting training costs. But current training is rather like a 'patchwork quilt', with variations according to the police service a recruit joins. There has been a proliferation in pre- and post-entry programmes too, including foundation degrees and National Vocational Qualification (NVQ). Some pre-entry study programmes require students to join the special constabulary to gain appropriate practice-based skills which are then accredited against the IPLDP, thus reducing time that would otherwise have been spent in the classroom. Unfortunately, some of these programmes have no recognised value within the service's training framework and many police services do not provide a dispensation for qualifications gained on other schemes.

# The Initial Police Learning and Development Programme

During the first two years of service, all police recruits undertake an extensive two-year training programme which combines formal training, closely tutored patrol

**Table 2.1** *Core responsibilities and activities of a patrol officer (patrol officer: integrated competency framework (ICF) – 2009 version 10).*

| Core responsibility | Activities |
| --- | --- |
| **Community safety** | |
| Conduct patrol | Respond to calls and requests for assistance, countering criminal activity and public disorder and minimising risks to public safety |
| Respond to road-related incidents, hazards, offences and collisions | Respond to traffic hazards, attend collision scenes and deal with traffic offences |
| **Police operations** | |
| Prepare for and participate in planned policing operations | Participate in police and agency-led operations, carrying out tasks in accordance with legislation and procedure |
| Provide an initial response to incidents | Respond promptly and take control of an incident, taking appropriate action to ensure that it is dealt with correctly |
| **Custody and prosecution** | |
| Custody procedures – arresting officer | Ensure the security and welfare of the detained person and lawfully comply with custody procedures |
| Conduct lawful arrest procedures | Carry out lawful arrests while having regard for the human rights, security and health and safety of the detainee |
| Prepare and submit case files | Prepare and submit case materials, working with CPS or other relevant agencies/organisations |
| Present evidence in court | Attend court and give evidence |
| **Intelligence** | |
| Use information to support policing objectives | Use information/intelligence to support achievement of community safety and crime reduction objectives |
| | Ensure that intelligence is used ethically and in accordance with legislation, policy, protocols and codes and practice |
| **Health, safety and welfare** | |
| Provide first aid | Identify the nature of illness or injury and provide the necessary first aid treatment in accordance with approved procedures |
| **Personal responsibility** | |
| Maintain standards of professional practice | Ensure that behaviour complies with organisational values |
| Promote equality, diversity and human rights | Promote equality, diversity and human rights by developing and maintaining positive working relationships |
| | Ensure that colleagues are treated fairly |
| | Contribute to developing equality of opportunity in work practices |
| Work as part of a team | Work with colleagues, contributing positively and constructively to the achievement of team and organisational objectives |

and formal assessment during the independent patrol phase. Learning and development is achieved through a variety of methods including facilitated group discussions, e-learning, individual and group exercises, presentations, simulated exercises, knowledge checks, workplace coaching and mentoring. The IPLDP also includes aspects of other police learning programmes, for example, Professionalising the Investigation Process Level 1, Equality and Human Rights and Mental Ill Health. In January 2010, the 'Diploma in Policing' was introduced as the standard minimum national qualification for the IPLDP. Within the diploma, 16 occupational standards are assessed with a further five being embedded throughout:

1. Communicate effectively.

2. Race and diversity.

3. Health and safety risk assessment.

4. Use law enforcement in a fair and justified way.

5. Maintain skills and knowledge.

---

**REFLECTIVE TASK**

*There has been a long-standing academic debate about what constitutes a 'profession'.*

*Whether or not police officers need a degree is therefore, at best, a moot point.*

*Discuss this with friends and family and decide whether higher education advances the professional status of policing or this is just 'intellectual snobbery'.*

---

# The special constable

Providing a uniform presence on streets and in public places is no longer the sole preserve of the police service. There has been a growth in the presence of privately funded security patrols and more recently a variety of warden schemes involving local authorities and other agencies using paid staff and volunteers. Indeed, the notion of volunteering is not new. Routh (1972, page 72) notes that *throughout history, there have been individuals willing to give of themselves in time, effort, resources and money to help their fellow man*. Contributions come in many forms: hospice voluntary workers, victim support workers, blood donors and a wide range of charities and, in the context of the United Kingdom police service, the special constable.

Specials have a long and impressive history, and the constabulary is seen by many as a vital part of modern-day policing. As of 31 March 2010, there were some 15,505 special constables representing about 9 per cent of the number of full-time equivalent regular officers (Home Office, 2010b). According to figures, the special constabulary is more representative of the community than the regular police service, not only by gender and ethnic background but by socio-economic group (NPIA, 2008). It also brings local knowledge and a rich mix of skills and talents, which is critical to enhancing the levels of service provided by the police and increasing public satisfaction.

However, the police service is facing uncharted territory in which the landscape is rapidly changing and highly uncertain. Faced with swinging cuts to police budgets, some services have all but stopped police officer recruitment. Unsurprisingly, many are seeking to make greater use of special constables and with demands to see the 'front line' bolstered, the role of the special constable has been brought into sharp relief. Community policing remains high on political agendas and with the 2012 London Olympics looming ever closer, attention has turned to volunteers to provide that front-line presence. This has also led to calls for further professionalisation of the role and a more corporate approach in areas such as recruitment, training, performance and leadership.

> ... there is a need to ensure a more consistent, national approach to special constabulary recruitment, induction, training and deployment practice to help professionalise the role and to further enhance their mobility and flexibility as a resource ...

> (HMIC, 2004, para 7.101)

Prior to such calls, the 43 police services were each responsible for the recruitment and training of special constables. Variations in processes and standards resulted in the launch of the National Strategy for the Special Constabulary in March 2008. This was to provide greater consistency in key areas such as marketing, recruitment, assessment, training and development, performance management, leadership, deployment and tasking. Roll out began in April 2010 and continued until March 2011. At the heart of the strategy is a standard core syllabus – the Initial Learning for Special Constables (IL4SC) – which is designed such that prior learning can be recognised at some future point. This should increase the opportunity for specials to work with any police service, as well as allow them to transfer into the regular service, or serve as community support officers (CSO). The basic training requirement for a special is approximately 120 hours which is undertaken at weekends and evenings. Successful candidates are attested and receive their warrant cards after swearing the oath of a constable.

---

REFLECTIVE TASK

*Some police services are planning to draw police recruits from within the ranks of their special constabulary. After gaining independent patrol status and a qualification in relevant law and policing, special constables will then be eligible to join the regular service. External applicants will be required to finance the course themselves, through local colleges.*

*Consider these proposals and decide whether they are likely to discriminate against people from diverse backgrounds, for example, single parents and older people, primary carers and those on low income. Or, do you think this is consistent with*

*REFLECTIVE TASK CONTINUED*

*the national modernisation agenda? For example, improving local service provisions and providing special constables with a range of transferable skills. Write down any other issues and considerations that spring to mind.*

# Special constable – qualifications and recruitment into the role

Any UK or Commonwealth citizen aged between 18.5 and 50 years, whose stay in the country is not limited, can apply to join the special constabulary. There are only a few occupations deemed to be incompatible with being a special constable such as working in public contact positions in the private security industry for which there would be a conflict of interest.

The national Specials Recruit Assessment Process involves the observation of a candidate's performance across a number of exercises to assess their potential to perform the role effectively.

Assessment exercises include:

- an optional competency-based questionnaire for police services that wish to sift prior to running further assessments;

- a written exercise lasting 20 minutes;

- a situational judgement test lasting 75 minutes;

- a competency-based structured interview with four questions lasting 20 minutes in total.

(NPIA, 2010)

All assessment exercises are based on standards within the ICF which you may recall describe the skills that are required for each police role, including that of a special constable. Briefly, this includes the following.

## Team working

Strong working relationships are important both inside and outside the policing team. Specials should, therefore, be able to support others in achieving team goals and a healthy work ethic.

## Community and customer focus

Specials are expected to understand and respond to the communities in which they work and show a commitment to policing which reflects the community's needs and concerns.

## Respect for race and diversity

Whatever the race, religion, position, background, circumstances, status or appearance of others may be, specials need to understand and respond appropriately to the views, opinions, circumstances and feelings of others. This is particularly important in areas of social, cultural and racial differences.

## Personal responsibility

Specials are required to act with integrity at all times and demonstrate motivation, commitment, perseverance and conscientiousness. They are also expected to assume responsibility for their personal behaviour and use initiative for resolving issues and problems.

## Resilience

This is important, particularly when making difficult decisions. Specials are expected to have the confidence to see their decisions through to a conclusion. They are expected to act appropriately at all times, be confident in their performance and act independently in normal circumstances.

---

*REFLECTIVE TASK*

*Individual case studies show clear evidence that specials deployed in challenging specialist or responsible roles serve longer than those deployed in less demanding tasks. Consider what type(s) of deployment(s) is/are appropriate within the role and the skills that are required to perform them effectively. You might wish to refer to the ICF Special Constabulary framework accessed via the following link:* www.npia.police.uk/en/docs/SpecialsICF.pdf

---

# Special constable – deployment and tasking

Most special constables work a minimum of four hours per week, typically evenings or weekends and wear uniforms similar to regular officers. Their principal role is to provide 'added value' support to the regular police service. This is achieved primarily through local, intelligence-based patrols and crime reduction initiatives, targeted at specific local crime problems in alignment with neighbourhood policing and the citizen focus agenda (NPIA, 2008).

The National Strategy recommends those tasks that should be allocated to the Special Constabulary. They are neither prescriptive nor exclusive and are considered to be within the capabilities of appropriately trained constables. They include:

- crime reduction tasks, for example, anti-vandal patrols to protect vulnerable properties and joint patrols of car boot sales with trading standards;

- public reassurance tasks, for example, crowd and traffic control at football and rugby matches and supporting Safer Neighbourhood teams through ASB and 'nuisance patrols' in targeted hotspots;

- investigation of minor crime;

- traffic offence reduction including drunken driving, speed enforcement using laser detection devices, checks of vehicle tyres and lights as part of road safety campaigns, detecting mobile phone and seat belt offences;

- automatic number-plate recognition vehicle stops;

- arrest of persons – on warrant – who have failed to appear in court;

- taking of elimination fingerprints at acquisitive crime scenes.

(NPIA, 2008)

# Community support officer

Some police services refer to these staff as 'police community support officers'. Although the terms are interchangeable, the name 'community support officers' is used throughout this chapter.

Increases in demand, along with competing priorities such as the need to respond quickly to urgent calls, has meant that the police have become increasingly mobile which has reduced their visibility and accessibility to the public. The Police Reform Act, 2002, now permits the appointment of CSOs with sufficient powers to deal with a variety of patrol tasks. This has led to an increase in the police service presence, thereby providing additional reassurance to the public (Home Office, 2004). Indeed, since March 2010, some 16,918 CSOs had been appointed which has enabled police officers to undertake more specialised tasks (Home Office, 2010b).

## CSO – qualifications and recruitment into the role

In April 2006, the Home Office introduced a national application form and selection centres for consistency in recruiting standards. Though individual police services are able to choose whether they use regional centres, actual assessment is based on a cluster of behaviours taken from the ICF.

The process involves the observation of performance across a variety of exercises which include:

- two interactive role-play exercises, lasting five minutes each;

- two written exercises, lasting 20 minutes each;

- a competency-based structured interview, comprising four questions, each lasting five minutes.

Although currently part of the Wider Police Learning and Development Programme, future CSO training is likely to align closely with the IPLDP. This will see the integration of 'common learning', thus allowing for the accreditation of prior learning.

This is reflected in the certificate in policing qualification which was introduced in June 2010, albeit this is a non-mandatory award. Because four of the award units are linked with the IPLDP, this provides opportunities for the recognition of prior learning for CSOs aspiring to become police officers.

## CSO – role and responsibilities

CSOs have the capacity to engage with the public and help tackle neighbourhood concerns, particularly low-level crime and ASB. The core role of the CSO is to provide reassurance through visible patrol and direct contact, for example, by attending community meetings, by street briefings and by carrying out face-to-face resident surveys. Unlike police officers, CSOs do not have general powers to arrest, but chief officers have the discretion to delegate any one of a number of powers: to carry out road checks, to seize controlled drugs and remove abandoned vehicles, to issue fixed penalty notices for specified offences that include littering and cycling on the footpath and the confiscation of alcohol and tobacco under specified conditions. It is through this type of activity that policing becomes familiar, accessible and visible to the public, and this is essential to promote feelings of safety, with uniformed foot patrol being the most effective (Home Office, 2007). Although chief officers have local discretion on how to develop the CSO role, the Association of Chief Police Officers has provided guidance by stating that CSOs should:

> *…contribute to the policing of neighbourhoods, primarily through highly visible patrol with the purpose of reassuring the public, increasing orderliness in public places and being accessible to communities and partner agencies working at local level. The emphasis of this role, and the powers required to fulfil it, will vary from neighbourhood to neighbourhood and force to force.*
> (Association of Chief Police Officers, 2005a)

CSOs are now firmly established in neighbourhood teams across England and Wales, working alongside constables, special constables and volunteers from partner organisations, for example, housing managers, youth workers and private security and neighbourhood watch groups, and together, they are responsible for addressing community issues.

The ICF goes further by defining the core responsibilities and activities of a CSO, some of which are listed in Table 2.2.

Let us now sum up the role of the CSO which is to promote public satisfaction and reassurance through visible patrol and by supplementing the police effort. Also remember that for the sake of clarity, CSOs have a limited number of powers and tasks, outside of which they should neither stray nor be expected to. For example, a CSO might reasonably observe an offence and call for support rather than personally intervene and detain. CSO activity should also be directed through the National Intelligence Model which is not exclusively about crime intelligence but is also applicable to community intelligence.

Special constables are expected to do much the same work as regular officers but on a part-time, voluntary basis. They generally work within a neighbourhood

*Table 2.2 Core responsibilities and activities of a community support officer (patrol officer: integrated competency framework (ICF) – 2009 version 10)*

| Core responsibility | Activities |
| --- | --- |
| **Community safety** | |
| Adopt a problem-solving approach | Take steps to deal with community issues, while understanding cause and effect – be able to work with others in providing solutions |
| Conduct patrol | Communicate effectively and provide appropriate help and support. Respond promptly to requests for police assistance. Identify and prevent risks to public safety, for example, potential public disorder. Use police powers in accordance with legislation and organisational policy |
| Promote and raise awareness of social responsibilities and community safety among young people | Work with schools, local community representatives and agency stakeholders to develop and implement initiatives that will educate young people on personal safety and crime awareness |
| **Intelligence** | |
| Gather and use intelligence to support policing objectives | Lawfully and ethically gather intelligence to facilitate the achievement of crime and disorder reduction objectives |
| **Police operations** | |
| Contribute to planned police operations | Participate in police and agency-led operations, carrying out tasks necessary for the successful implementation of the operation while acting in accordance with legislation and procedure |
| Provide an initial response | Respond promptly and follow procedures for the type of incident, prioritising your actions |
| | Record accurate details |
| | Consider your safety and that of others at the scene |
| | Attend to casualties at the scene, taking account of personal safety, providing first aid where appropriate |
| **Investigation** | |
| Conduct an investigation | Conduct the investigation and preserve scene |
| Provide care for victims and witnesses | Demonstrate support for victims and witnesses and recognise any possible impact on the community |
| Search persons or personal property | Search individual(s) or personal property in accordance with legislation, policy and procedures |
| **Custody and prosecution** | |
| Prepare and submit case files | Ensure that the process of information is carried out promptly and efficiently in accordance with legislation, policy and procedure |

*Table 2.2 (Continued)*

| Core responsibility | Activities |
| --- | --- |
| Present evidence in court and at other hearings | Attend court and give evidence in accordance with legislation |
| **Managing and organisation** | |
| Participate in meetings | Prepare for, and actively contribute in a clear, concise and relevant manner, ensuring that decisions and actions are communicated to appropriate personnel |
| Provide specialist advice and knowledge | Provide specialist advice and knowledge to colleagues, partners and other individuals and agencies |
| **Health, safety and welfare** | |
| Provide first aid | Identify the nature of illness or injury and provide the necessary first aid treatment in accordance with approved procedures |
| **Managing and developing people** | |
| Prepare and deliver presentations | Prepare and deliver using an appropriate communication style |

policing framework along with police officers, CSOs and partners from a range of organisations. Crucially, they have the same police powers as regular constables but primarily operate according to the nature of the neighbourhood and the priorities for the area.

**CHAPTER SUMMARY**

This chapter has focussed on the recruitment process, training of police constables, special constables and CSOs along with the key skills and qualities of these roles. We have argued that policing, once characterised by a doctrine of independence, has become less insulated from central- and local-government control. The Police Reform and Social Responsibility Bill aims to restore this independence and to reconnect the police and the public by reducing targets and giving the public a direct say on how neighbourhoods should be policed. This is particularly important as the public become worried about 'deviancy' and more fearful of the risk of victimisation. It is here that we made the 'inexorable link' with local, neighbourhood policing and a reserve army of volunteers prepared to act as community crime fighters – the special constable. Their principal role is to provide 'added value' support to the regular police service primarily through local, intelligence-based patrols and crime reduction initiatives. These efforts have been bolstered by the CSOs and their powers to deal with a variety of patrol tasks. This has increased the police service presence through visibility and accessibility and has brought about the additional reassurance to the public.

You will also recall that SFJ is responsible for ensuring that those working within the justice sector have the appropriate skills to do their job. Structured activities listed within a competency framework provide role definition and guidance on recruitment, registers of competence, promotion and career progression. Entry to the police service is open to almost everyone provided that selection procedures are met. This is currently followed by a two-year training programme – the IPLDP – which some police services run in conjunction with higher education providers. There has been a proliferation in pre- and post-entry programmes including foundation degrees and NVQs some of which require students to join the special constabulary in anticipation that this will reduce the time that would otherwise have been spent in the classroom. Unfortunately, many of these programmes have no recognised value within the services' training framework. Indeed, many police services do not provide a dispensation for qualifications gained on other schemes which has placed formal education and the notion of 'professionalism' under the spotlight – as stated, whether or not police officers need formal qualifications or a degree is therefore a point for discussion.

---

*CASE STUDY*

*Having identified some of the roles and responsibilities of the patrol officer, special constable and CSO, the case study is now used to provide additional context.*

*You will recall that foot patrol officers had been deployed to the scene of a robbery at a town centre shop. First response officers and a special constable had also been deployed in a police van along with the air support helicopter and armed response vehicle; it is believed that one of the suspects was carrying a firearm at the time of the robbery. While the offenders initially fled on foot, the police have information that suggests the suspects had access to a stolen motor vehicle. A small crowd has gathered at the scene and the first response officers have requested 'back up' from the town centre neighbourhood policing team ....*

*Put yourself in the position of one of the police responders and think about your initial response. You should be aware that a poor or inadequate investigation will do little to reassure the local community. Likewise, it can have an adverse impact on the standards of service that victims and witnesses are entitled to. The investigation should aim to maximise the amount of material that is collected and doing this quickly will increase the chances of preserving any evidence. The 'golden hour' is a term used to describe the period immediately following the commission of an offence, when evidence should be readily available to the police and it follows that positive action in the golden hour can minimise the attrition of material and increase the chances of locating witnesses.*

*(Association of Chief Police Officers, 2005b, para 4.2.2)*

*Now consider the following elements of an investigation.*

## The scene

- *Assess the factors likely to impact the investigation and take appropriate action to minimise risk.*
- *Identify and take appropriate steps to secure and preserve the scene(s) for future examination, for example, by the Scenes of Crime Officer and photographer.*
- *Take care not to contaminate the scene(s) or the potential evidence.*
- *For serious offences, consider cordoning off the scene and commencing a record of those arriving, entering and/or leaving the scene.*
- *Identify the need for any specialist support required to assist or advise in the gathering of evidence.*
- *Where appropriate, seize exhibits.*

## Victims and witnesses

- *Identify victims and potential witnesses and list the evidence they can provide.*
- *List who else a statement would be needed from and why.*
- *Document, photograph injuries and ensure forensic evidence is obtained.*
- *Obtain statement(s) while details are fresh in the mind of the witness.*
- *Conduct enquiries at adjacent premises with result, negative or positive.*
- *Ensure that victims and witnesses are kept informed of the progress of the investigation, and provided with any necessary support and protection.*
- *Take steps to minimise the potential negative impact that the incident might have on the local community.*

## Identify the suspect

- *Comprehensively record and circulate the description of the suspect(s).*
- *Record any actions you have taken to trace this suspect.*
- *Recover CCTV evidence at or near the scene and exhibit it.*
- *Record any other CCTV evidence you have not yet obtained.*

CASE STUDY *continued*

*Prioritise the above and create a list of tasks for those attending; these should reflect, and be appropriate for, the role. You should be able to justify the order of the tasks and why they are appropriate for the individual. Consider and identify any other tasks not listed.*

## Self-assessment questions

1. When was the 'Policing Pledge' rescinded and why?

2. Which organisation is responsible for ensuring that those working within the justice sector have the appropriate skills to do their job?

3. What is the Integrated Competency Framework?

4. Identify some of the methods used in the IPLDP to achieve learning and development.

5. What is the name of the standard minimum national qualification for the IPLDP?

6. What assessment exercises are included in the specials recruitment process?

7. Name four tasks which the national strategy suggests are within the capability of an appropriately trained special constable.

8. What are neighbourhood teams?

9. What is the 'golden hour'?

10. What factors are likely to impact the investigation of the robbery?

*FURTHER READING*

Cox, P (2010) *Passing the Police Recruit Assessment Process*, 2nd edition. Exeter: Learning Matters.

McMunn, R (2010) *How to Become a Police Community Support Officer (PCSO): The Insider's Guide*. Glasgow: Bell and Bain Limited.

McTaggard, J (2010) *The Definitive Guide to Passing the Police Recruitment Process: A Handbook for Prospective Police Officers, Special Constables and Police Community Support Officers*. Oxford: How To Books Limited.

Newburn, T (2007) *Criminology*. Devon: Willan Publishing.

Rogers, C and Lewis, R (2007) *Introduction to Police Work*. Devon: Willan Publishing.

**REFERENCES**

Association of Chief Police Officers (1994) *Working Party on Policing Standards Report*. London: ACPO.

Association of Chief Police Officers (2005a) *Guidance on Police Community Support Workers*. Revised June, 2005. London: ACPO.

Association of Chief Police Officers (2005b) *Practice Advice on Core Investigative Doctrine*. Available online at www.ssiacymru.org.uk/media/pdf/6/c/Core_Investigation_Doctrine_Interactive_1_.pdf (accessed 19 September 2010).

Belbin, M (2010) *Management Teams: Why They Succeed or Fail*, 3rd edition. Burlington, MA: Butterworth Heinemann.

Blaug, R, Horner, L and Lekhi, R (2006a:46) *Public Value, Citizen Expectations and User Commitment: A Literature Review*. London: The Work Foundation.

Cohen, S (2002) *Folk Devils and Moral Panics, 30th anniversary edition*. London: Routledge.

Consumer Focus (2010) *Public Call for Police to Improve Standard of Customer Service*. Available online at www.consumerfocus.org.uk/news/public-call-for-police-to-improve-standard-of-customer-service (accessed 12 November 2010).

Critchley, T A (1978) *A History of the Police in England and Wales*. London: Constable.

Goldstein, H (1990) *Problem Orientated Policing*. New York: McGraw-Hill.

HMIC (2004) *Modernising the Police Service: A Thematic Inspection of Workforce Modernisation – The Role, Management and Deployment of Police Staff in the Police Service in England and Wales*. Available online at www.hmic.gov.uk/sitecollectiondocuments/archive/arc_20040101.pdf (accessed 3 July 2010).

HMIC (2008) *Neighbourhood Policing/Citizen Focus, Part 2*. Available online at www.hmic.gov.uk/inspections/programmedinspections/pages/phase2%28neighbourhoodpolicingandcitizenfocus%29.aspx (accessed 18 October 2008).

HMIC (2009) *Responsive Policing; Delivering the Policing Pledge*. Available online at www.hmic.gov.uk/sitecollectiondocuments/policing%20pledge%20inspections/ppi_nfs_20090930.pdf (accessed 9 October 2010).

Home Office (2002) *Training Matters*. Available online at www.hmic.gov.uk/sitecollectiondocuments/archive/arc_20020101.pdf (accessed 3 October 2010).

Home Office (2004) *Building Communities, Beating Crime: A Better Police Service for the 21st Century*. London: HMSO.

Home Office (2007) *A National Evaluation of Community Support Officers, Homer Office Research Study, 297*. London: HMSO.

Home Office (2010a) *Policing in the 21st Century: Reconnecting Police and the People*. London: HMSO.

Home Office (2010b) *Statistical Bulletin; Police Service Strength, England and Wales, 31 March 2010*. London: HMSO.

IPLDP Central Authority (2004) *Programme Documentation: IPLDP Central Authority Terms of Reference*. Vol. 1.1, 24 January. London: Home Office.

Mayhew, P and Hough, M (1988) The British Crime Survey; Origins and Impact, in Maguire, M and Ponting, J (eds), *Victims of Crime: a New Deal*. Milton Keynes: OUP.

NPIA (2008) *Special Constabulary National Strategy Implementation Advice*. Available online at www.npia.police.uk/en/docs/Imp_Strategy_updated.pdf (accessed 2 August 2010).

NPIA (2010) *Specials Recruitment*. Available online at www.npia.police.uk/en/13930.htm (accessed 13 September 2010).

Peak, K and Glensor, R W (1996) Implementing Change: Community-Oriented Policing and Problem Solving. *FBI Law Enforcement Bulletin*, 65(7): 14–21.

Philips, D (1983) A Just Measure of Crime, Authority, Hunters and Blue Locusts; The 'Revisionist' Social History of Crime and the Law in Britain 1780–1850, in Cohen, S and Scull, A (eds), *Social Control and the State*. Oxford: Martin Robertson.

Routh, T A (1972) *The Volunteer and Community Agencies*. Chicago, IL: Charles Thomas Press.

Skills for Justice (2009) Integrated Competency, version 10. Available online at www.skillsforjustice.com (accessed 19 November 2010).

Tuckman B W (1965) Developmental Sequence in Small Groups. *Psychological Bulletin* 63: 384–99.

Wright, M and Waddington, P A J (2010) *What is Policing*. Exeter: Learning Matters.

# 3 The forensic investigation

HELEN PEPPER

### CHAPTER OBJECTIVES

By the end of this chapter you will have:

• developed knowledge and understanding of the recruitment, training and roles of the crime scene investigator, chemical enhancement technician, forensic photographer, fingerprint examiner and forensic computer analyst;

• understood the key skills and expectations of each role;

• understood the recruitment into these roles.

## Introduction

This chapter explores some of the roles within the forensic and crime scene arena.

• Crime scene investigator.

• Fingerprint examiner.

• Chemical enhancement technician.

• Forensic photographer.

• Forensic computer analyst.

Fans of TV crime drama often think that all the 'forensic' work is done by one individual, who solves the case, arrests the guilty and obtains a confession – usually within the space of a one-hour episode!

This is, however, not the case; there are many distinct areas of expertise which require different attributes in those aspiring to do the work.

# Background

Forensic investigation of crime, as we know it today, has evolved over hundreds of years. The first forensic scientists were doctors who were called to examine the body at the scene of a death. A Chinese book from 1248 talks about the injuries to and marks left on the neck which could identify death by strangulation (Nickell and Fischer, 1999).

But it was not until the early twentieth century that the scientific examination of crime scenes was introduced when Edmond Locard opened his police laboratory in Lyons. In 1920, Locard published his exchange principle that states that whenever two objects come into contact, something will be exchanged from one to the other. Locard's exchange principle is the basis of forensic investigation (Sutton and Trueman, 2009).

# Modern forensic services

From these early beginnings modern forensic investigation has grown into a service utilised on a daily basis to detect crimes ranging from simple thefts to murder and terrorism.

Each of the UK's Home Office police forces has a specialist scientific support department whose staff attend scenes of crime and gather evidence, take and process photographs and identify fingerprints. There are also independent specialist forensic science providers who analyse physical evidence recovered from crime scenes, perform DNA analysis and many other specialist tasks.

If you want to work within the forensic arena, you need to have an understanding of the different job roles, what each role entails and where the job holder would be employed.

The structure of a police scientific support department was established mainly as a result of a review carried out by Touche Ross Management Consultants on behalf of the Home Office (Touche Ross, 1987). The department head is the scientific support manager who controls the day-to-day running of the department, including the scenes of crime, fingerprints (including chemical enhancement unit) and photography sections. Each section will have its own head who will normally be an experienced specialist from within the discipline.

Usually, the fingerprint and photographic sections will be based at a central location, with crime scene investigation staff being based at police stations throughout the force area.

Fingerprints recovered from crime scenes are analysed and identified in fingerprint bureaux within police forces. All other forensic analyses and comparisons are done in a forensic science laboratory. Forensic science laboratories are independent commercial companies that are employed by the police to provide forensic services. The largest company in the United Kingdom presently is LGC Forensics, which employs over 500 staff (LGC Forensics, 2011), but there are several other companies that do general forensic work, as well as companies that specialise in 'niche' areas such as computer analysis or mobile phone interrogation.

Now that we have an understanding of the structure of forensic services in the United Kingdom, we will now examine some of the roles in more detail.

# Crime scene investigator/volume crime scene investigator

The job title of crime scene investigator (CSI) is a fairly new one in the United Kingdom. Previously, the role had been called scenes of crime officer (SOCO), scientific support officer or sometimes scientific aids officer, and these titles are still used in some forces. The name change came about as a result of a report called 'Using Forensic Science Effectively' (ACPO/FSS, 1996) which proposed that the role of SOCOs should be as part of the investigation team, and that it was not unreasonable to consider them as investigators in their own right. This idea was consolidated by the Police Reform Act (Great Britain Parliament, 2002), a piece of legislation which gave chief constables the power to devolve certain police powers to civilian employees. SOCOs were designated with investigatory powers by most forces and as a result their job name changed to crime scene investigator.

## Job description

A generic job description for a CSI is given below. This gives us some idea of what the police would look for in a potential employee.

## Job purpose

- To attend scenes of incidents and recover physical evidence, including taking photographs or video where necessary to provide a record of the scene.

- To act as a source of intelligence, linking crime scenes together and offenders to scenes by accurate and detailed recording of the modus operandi and the maintenance of databases of footwear marks and so forth.

- To detect and recover fingerprints and palm prints from the crime scene.

- The packaging and storage of physical evidence to prevent loss, contamination or deterioration.

- To give advice on forensic matters to others involved in the investigative process.

- To prepare witness statements, and be present at court to give evidence where necessary.

(ACPO/FSS, 1996)

## Core work areas

A CSI will attend crime scenes (and sometimes other incidents such as road traffic collisions or industrial accidents) at the request of the investigating officer to recover physical evidence.

When at the crime scene, the CSI will wear an appropriate level of personal protective equipment and ensure others within the scene do so if necessary, both to protect health and safety and to minimise the risk of evidence within the scene becoming contaminated.

They will make detailed notes which include details of the date, time and location they have attended, who was present, any information supplied about the incident and a detailed modus operandi. The notes will also include a sketch plan and list any evidence recovered. The CSI will normally use a digital camera to make a photographic record of the scene.

When the CSI recovers evidence, they will ensure that it is recovered, packaged and stored in such a way as to maintain its integrity as a piece of evidence and to prevent it becoming lost, damaged or contaminated.

They will generate and record intelligence information to assist the investigations, and liaise with others specialists, such as the local intelligence unit (see Chapter 5), with regard to intelligence matters.

The CSI will also prepare witness statements detailing the crime scene examinations they have conducted, and then, if required, attend court (either a criminal court or coroner's court) to give evidence.

## Other duties

The CSI will often be called upon to give advice regarding forensic matters (such as the packaging of forensic exhibits) across the police force. On occasion they will also be required to provide training to other police officers, community support officers and the like, either by providing workshop sessions or by facilitating work experience.

A single job description cannot encompass all the requirements of such a varied job. The CSI will be required to carry out such other duties as may be determined from time to time within the general scope of the post.

## What does the role involve?

A CSI will normally work in a shift system that involves evening and weekend work on a regular basis. Night cover is provided by either the shift system or an 'on call' rota, whereby a CSI will standby at home but will respond to any calls through the night. Night call-outs are normally restricted to more serious scenes such as armed robbery or murder.

A routine shift will see the CSI attending shift briefings to gather information about the crime that has been occurring in their area and completing administrative tasks, but the majority of their time will be spent 'out and about' attending crime scenes such as burglaries, taking photographs of people who have injuries from being assaulted or examining recovered stolen motor vehicles.

Things can change at a moment's notice because if a serious crime is reported, the CSI will be required to re-prioritise their work to enable them to attend the serious crime scene as soon as possible and prevent evidence from being lost. So the CSI must be adaptable and cope well with changes at short notice.

## Volume crime scene investigator

In recent years, a new role has been introduced into scenes-of-crime work – that of the volume crime scene investigator (VCSI). The VCSI undertakes much the same routine tasks as the CSI, but they do not have the same level of training and are not allowed to work at serious crime scenes such as murders. Increasingly, the forces are recruiting people to the post of VCSI and then recruiting CSIs internally from the ranks of experienced VCSIs.

## Recruitment

As has been mentioned earlier, recruitment to a job in crime scene investigation is now most likely through the role of the VCSI. Jobs are advertised in the local press and on police force websites.

## Qualifications for recruitment as a CSI/VCSI

Recruitment as a CSI/VCSI does not necessarily require a high level of academic attainment, with the minimum requirement generally being GCSE English and maths grade C or above. A driving license is usually also required. It has to be said that competition for jobs is strong, so the minimum requirements will not normally be enough to secure an interview.

A successful candidate may well have a relevant higher qualification, such as an honours degree in crime scene science, forensic science or a photography qualification, or they could have relevant work experience, such as having worked within the criminal justice environment or served as a special constable.

## Skills and qualities

A VCSI/CSI should be methodical and meticulous and have an enquiring mind. They should have the ability to work alone or as part of a team and be prepared to work unsocial hours. The working conditions can be difficult, and a CSI is often required to deal with distressing incidents so they need a good degree of resilience.

A large part of the role involves talking to people, whether it is briefing investigators on findings or trying to draw out information about what has happened at a scene from a distraught victim, so exceptional communication skills are important. This is one area where the fictional portrayal of the CSI and the reality differs – on TV the CSI is always working in a scene where everyone else has been excluded. This would be an accurate representation of a major crime scene such as a murder, but most of the time, the CSI will be visiting scenes such as house burglaries, where the occupiers will be present. Being the victim of a crime is a deeply unpleasant experience, and the person may be feeling alternately angry and afraid, so the CSI must show tact and empathy and develop a thick skin as victims are prone to vent their frustrations on anyone at hand.

## Training

The Touche Ross (1987) report highlighted that the training of scenes-of-crime personnel varied greatly from force to force and recommended that a standardised training package be developed to cover the core elements of fingerprint and forensic evidence recovery and basic photography (Pepper, 2010).

CSIs undertake a training course that lasts between 8 and 12 weeks and cover the areas recommended by Touche Ross. The main providers of these courses to the Home Office police forces are the National Training Centre for Scientific Support to Crime Investigation run by the National Policing Improvement Agency (NPIA) in County Durham, and the Crime Academy run by the Metropolitan Police Service.

VCSIs receive a much shorter three- to four-week training course, covering the same elements, but not in as great a depth. They can, at a later date, complete a 'conversion course' to qualify as a CSI.

On successful completion of the training course, VCSIs/CSIs undergo a tutorship period, where they work with an experienced officer until they are deemed competent to operate on their own and can undertake study to qualify themselves further.

A VCSI/CSI will need to drive a police vehicle to travel to scenes. Most forces require anyone who will drive a police vehicle as part of their duties to undergo driver's training and take a police driving test. Scenes-of-crime personnel do not need to use 'blues and twos' when driving and are therefore not trained as response drivers, but will normally be expected to perform at the level of a Department of transport advanced driver.

## Career progression

Career progression within crime scene work is hampered by the number of vacancies (Pepper, 2010). We have already mentioned that suitably experienced VCSIs can progress to the role of a CSI.

Each scenes-of-crime unit will normally have a senior CSI who has responsibility for the day-to-day management of the office and supervisory responsibility for the CSIs based there. To become a senior CSI, you would normally need between two and five years' experience as a CSI, should have completed further qualifications such as the diploma in crime scene investigation and possibly undergone some management training.

In addition to the supervisory role of senior CSI, progression is also possible by completing further training to qualify as a crime scene manager (CSM). The CSM takes a supervisory role at major crime scenes, directing a team of CSIs within the scene (Sutton and Trueman, 2009).

Qualified CSMs can complete further training to become a crime scene co-ordinator. Co-ordinators work as part of the senior management team at major incidents where there are multiple scenes. They do not attend any of the scenes but direct the forensic response and act as forensic advisors to the investigation, working closely with the senior investigating officer (see Chapter 4). They also act as liaison between the investigation and independent forensic service providers.

There is scope for development within the role, with some CSIs attaining specialisations in areas such as fire investigation or footwear mark comparison. Some forces also have a dedicated forensic trainer, and this is a role that an experienced CSI could undertake.

# Fingerprint examiner

In 1900, a Home Office committee known as the Belper Committee sat to explore the merits of using fingerprints as a system of identification (Beavan, 2003). Following the committee's recommendations, the first fingerprint bureau in the United Kingdom was opened by the Metropolitan Police on 1 July 1901(McCartney, 2006). By 1932, the fingerprint bureau at New Scotland Yard held over half a million sets of fingerprints and made over 20,000 identifications a year (Henry, 1934).

Today, fingerprint classification and identification is done by fingerprint officers working in force fingerprint bureaux throughout the United Kingdom.

Fingerprint examiners classify and compare fingerprints found at crime scenes with those held on record, with the intention of identifying the person who left the fingerprints at the scene. The work demands close attention to detail and a high degree of precision. Fingerprint searches can be done manually, using a magnifying glass to compare fingerprints from scenes with those of known persons held on record, or by use of an automated computer system known as Ident1.

The role of the fingerprint examiner is generally divided into two grades – trainee fingerprint officer (trainee) and expert fingerprint officer (expert), and both roles will be described in the job description below.

## Job purpose

- Trainee: To acquire in-depth expertise in all aspects of fingerprint identification techniques and to obtain 'expert' status by completing a structured training programme and during this three- to- five-year training period, to provide an identification service to operational staff, under the direction of a supervisor.

- Expert: To provide an accurate and efficient fingerprint identification service, to assist in the detection of offences and the prosecution of offenders.

## Core work areas

The trainee identifies persons by means of fingerprints and palm prints using both manual and computerised fingerprint systems. They update and interrogate the Ident1 computerised fingerprint identification system and prepare statements of evidence for use in court. They may also attend court to give evidence.

Trainees also prepare and give presentations to staff and visitors on the role of the fingerprint bureau in detecting crime and identifying offenders.

They must also endeavour to develop their skills by attending and successfully completing training courses and work-based learning events with the ultimate goal of obtaining 'expert' status.

An expert is responsible for achieving the maximum number of fingerprint identifications possible utilising their knowledge, experience, skill and expertise. They then act as an 'expert witness' and present non-factual evidence of opinion to High, Crown, Magistrates and Coroners Courts across England and Wales. Experts advise operational officers, crown prosecution service, solicitors and barristers regarding identifications and guidelines covering standards for court. After numerous checks, they prepare their evidence in a clear and concise manner to ensure that miscarriages of justice do not occur and subsequently an individual is not wrongly convicted.

---

### REFLECTIVE TASK

*Miscarriages of justice do occur owing to the misidentification of fingerprints. Such events have enormous implications for the fingerprint identification service as a whole. The case of Shirley McKie in Scotland during the late 1990s is a good example which led to a number of reforms in practice.*

*Look at www.guardian.co.uk/uk/2006/apr/18/ukcrime.features11 and consider how this affects your confidence in fingerprints as a form of forensic evidence*

(O'Neill, 2006)

---

Due to the extremely high standards required to be permitted to give evidence of opinion as opposed to fact in order to secure a conviction in court, fingerprint experts may now be required to undergo blind testing, competency appraisal, refresher courses and audits both internally and by an external QA audit team. Failure may entail removal from the national register of fingerprint experts.

## Qualifications

Generally, a trainee fingerprint officer is expected to be educated to 'A' level standard or its equivalent. To be recruited as an expert fingerprint officer, one must have passed the advanced fingerprint course and be enrolled on the national register of fingerprint experts.

## Skills and qualities

Fingerprint examiners should ideally have a good level of computer literacy and be competent in the use of Microsoft Word, Outlook and Excel, with good communication and interpersonal skills because they deal with police staff, outside organisations and other police forces on a daily basis. They need a retentive memory and enthusiasm for learning and development. Examiners must possess the ability to concentrate for long periods of time and have a good eye for detail, as well as be able to work with minimum supervision. Records need to be maintained accurately, and examiners need to be able to present information confidently and concisely.

## Training

The Association of Chief Police Officers-approved national fingerprint learning programme takes students from foundation to advanced level in three to five years. The training programme leads a fingerprint examiner through their career from trainee to expert status and on to continuous professional development.

The programme requires attendance on residential foundation and intermediate and advanced fingerprint assessment courses in addition to successful completion of evidential portfolios in the workplace. Fingerprint examiners who successfully achieve expert status are then included on the national register of fingerprint experts.

Once expert status has been reached, the fingerprint examiner is able to achieve and maintain competency within their role through external workshops, in-force training, distance learning and performance monitoring (NPIA, 2010a).

## Career progression

Progression from trainee to expert status is automatic on successful completion of the relevant training. However, once expert status is reached, the opportunity for further development is limited. There is some scope for attaining a supervisory role as team leader within the bureau or a management role as head of bureau, depending on the availability of posts.

# Chemical enhancement technician

Chemical enhancement technicians (also known as fingerprint development officers) work primarily in the fingerprint development laboratory and are responsible for the examination of articles recovered from crime scenes using specialist equipment, chemicals and techniques to find and enhance fingerprint marks which would often be invisible to the naked eye.

They do sometimes attend crime scenes, particularly major offences such as murder, to assist with the recovery of fingerprints.

Fingerprints can be left behind at crime scenes by the raised ridges, called 'friction ridges', found on the skin of the inner surface of the hand. Friction ridges are also found on the soles of the feet, and identification of 'foot' prints (known as plantar impressions) can be carried out in much the same way as fingerprint impressions. Along the raised surface of the ridges, there are over 550 sweat pores per square centimetre (Siegel et al., 2000) which allow the skin to cool by the discharge of sweat. The sweat is made up of approximately 98.5 per cent water and the remaining 1.5 per cent is made up of amino acids, chlorides, fats, sugars and urea (Pepper, 2010).

CSIs would use fingerprint powders (mainly aluminium powder although others are available) at crime scenes to search for and recover fingerprints. These powders work really well on clean, smooth, shiny surfaces such as glass or gloss-painted woodwork, but not so well on textured surfaces such as plain wood or most plastics. This is where the chemical enhancement technician comes in because it is the various constituents of that 1.5 per cent of sweat that can be made to react with various chemicals or glow under specialist lighting conditions to reveal the presence of fingerprints.

For example, gentian violet is a dye that binds to the fatty components of sweat, producing a strong purple fingerprint. Superglue fuming (cyanoacrylate vapour) works very well on lots of surfaces, including textured plastic and metal. The fumes from heated superglue are allowed to circulate around the item and settle on fingerprints in the form of a white deposit. High-intensity light sources can cause fingerprints to luminesce, making them visible, and there are many other chemical reactions and techniques available. Whatever the type of surface to be examined or the substance making up the fingerprint, the chemical enhancement technician will have an examination method to find, record and recover the fingerprints. However, many of the chemicals used and techniques employed can be hazardous to health, which is why the chemical enhancement technician does most of their analyses in the controlled environment of a laboratory.

## Job description

A generic job description for a chemical enhancement technician is given below. It will give us an idea of the qualifications, skills and attributes needed for the job.

## Job purpose

- To provide a 'laboratory service' to the Force in the examination of items submitted from CSIs and other sources (such as detectives), utilising modern laboratory techniques, and to preserve and develop evidence left by offenders at scenes of crime and other incidents.

- To use specialist equipment and chemical processes to develop and enhance latent or visible fingerprint impressions, and photographing and processing developed marks for submission to the fingerprint department for comparison and identification.

## Core work areas

The chemical enhancement technician can identify and select the best practice sequential methods for treatment of exhibits to locate, enhance and develop fingerprints. They understand the chemical constituents being used in relation to specific hazards and the associated general health and safety measures. They also understand the hazards involved in disposal of chemicals and ensure compliance with specific health and safety requirements. Chemical enhancement technicians are aware of the destructive capabilities of certain chemicals and procedures and ensure adequate consent has been obtained prior to their use.

The equipment and methods of photography, both digital and conventional wet photography, are utilised to record developed fingerprints, including the use of macro-photography and specialist lighting techniques. All technical equipment is maintained by the chemical enhancement technicians to the highest standards, and they ensure accurate calibration of the equipment to meet the need for evidential continuity and evidence integrity. As such they must maintain accurate records of all processes used, prepare witness statements and attend court to give evidence if and when required.

Chemical enhancement technicians ensure that necessary health and safety risk assessments are adhered to throughout and wear appropriate health and safety clothing and equipment, for example, when using the Quasar high-intensity light source and toxic or dangerous chemicals.

## Qualifications

There is no standard entry level, but an applicant would normally be expected to have English, maths and a science-based subject GCSEs at grade C or above. A recognised photography qualification is also quite often specified.

## Skills and qualities

Ideally, a chemical enhancement technician should have previous experience of working in a laboratory or technical environment and previous photography experience. Chemical enhancement technicians should be flexible and resourceful in their approach to their work and have good analytical and problem-solving skills. They also require good computer skills with competence in various IT software such as Microsoft Word, Outlook and Excel. They also need to have good written, verbal and interpersonal communication skills, as well as the ability to interact with police staff and other agencies on a regular basis.

## Training

On recruitment into the role, a chemical enhancement technician would be required to attend a two-week fingerprint evidence recording and retrieval (FERRT) course. This is a residential course held at the NPIA's site in County Durham.

The course participants work in the laboratory and carry out a range of chemical processes. The course has sessions conducted by the National Fingerprint Training and Home Office Scientific Development Branch (HOSDB). The course enables students to gain practical experience in the processes contained in the HOSDB manual of 'Fingerprint Development Techniques' and the use of high-intensity light sources to enhance and recover fingerprints.

After successfully completing the FERRT course and gaining experience in the workplace, chemical enhancement technicians can attend a FERRT Development Course, which gives them the opportunity to learn how to apply their skills at the crime scene (NPIA, 2010b).

## Career progression

Opportunities for career progression within the chemical enhancement laboratory are limited. Many police forces employ a single chemical enhancement technician, and where there is more than one, there is often no hierarchy. In some forces, it may be possible to progress to the role of supervisor, having supervisory responsibility for a limited number of chemical enhancement technicians.

# Forensic photographer

In most police forces, general crime-scene photography is done by CSIs, but some forces (notably the Metropolitan Police) still have forensic photographer as a distinct job role.

The role of the forensic photographer is very different from other commercial photography jobs. Police photographs are not a creative opportunity to show a scene or product at its artistic best, but rather a means of producing an accurate record of the crime scene or a piece of evidence as it was found. Photographs can also be useful in helping a witness to recall events or assist in clarifying statements in court (Warlen, 1995).

The forensic photographer will be one of the first technicians to arrive at a major crime scene. They will make a complete photographic record of the scene from every angle, taking long, intermediate and close-up views of anything that may be evidentially significant.

They will also attend post-mortems to photograph the deceased, the injuries and significant medical findings at the direction of the forensic pathologist, or photograph injuries to assault victims either at their home or in hospital. They may also attend road traffic collisions and work closely with the collision investigators to make a record of the collision scene and anything evidentially significant, such as apparent defects on the vehicles or skid marks on the road. Forensic photographers may also be utilised by their force on happier occasions – to take public relations photographs or photographs of visiting dignitaries.

Even in the police forces where CSIs do the majority of the photography, there will still be a photographic unit whose staff are responsible for developing, storing and printing images for court or display purposes. The photography unit will also be available to undertake more challenging specialist photography such as infrared photography of bite marks or ultraviolet photography of 'Smartwater' chemical marker activations.

## Recruitment into the role

Forensic photographers are often recruited from the ranks of established CSIs, but roles are sometimes advertised in the national press and in specialist journals such as *New Scientist*, *Police Review* and the *British Journal of Photography*.

## Job description

A generic job description for a forensic photographer is given below, to provide an idea of the qualifications, skills and aptitudes required for this role.

## Job purpose

- Forensic photographers produce a permanent visual record of the scenes of accidents and crime for use as evidence in court.

- They must be able to produce detailed recordings of all the available evidence at the scene, including overview photographs and accurate images of tire marks, fingerprints, footprints, blood spatters, bullet holes and other unique evidence at the scene.

- They must also be able to take detailed photographs of injuries sustained through accidents or assaults and may also be required to photograph dead bodies (Skillset, 2009).

- Photographers will also often be required to make video recordings of scenes, which can be used for briefing purposes during the investigation.

## Core work areas

A forensic photographer conducts general and specialist photography at crime scenes, road traffic collisions, post-mortems and other incidents using digital and video recording equipment. Other duties may include the taking of promotional and public relations photographs for the police force.

They are responsible for developing, storing and printing of the photographic images, including digital images.

A forensic photographer would need to be able to prepare witness statements and attend court to give evidence as and when required.

## Qualifications

Usually a BTEC National Diploma in Photography (or equivalent).

## Skills and qualities

A forensic photographer should be proficient in all types of photography – both traditional wet photography and digital photography – the use of video.

They should have previous experience of working in a technical photographic environment and be able to follow a standard methodology and produce images to a rigorous technical standard so that they can be used as evidence in hearings, tribunals and court proceedings.

A forensic photographer must be able to work with a minimum of supervision, quickly and efficiently without disturbing the crime scene. They will often be required to work in challenging and/or distressing environments and therefore must be resilient towards some of the sights they may witness.

## Training

A typical route to employment as a forensic photographer is to complete a recognised course in photography (e.g., City & Guilds or BTEC National Diploma in Photography) and to apply for jobs with police forces or specialist forensic service companies, taking advantage of subsequent on-the-job training.

There are also some specialist courses that deal with forensic photography and forensic imaging, as well as photo-imaging modules on forensic science degree courses. More specialised training in fingerprints, footwear, vehicle examination, lighting and documents is often conducted within the photographic units of the police forces or forensic science companies (Skillset, 2009).

## Career progression

There is very limited opportunity for career progression. In some forces, it may be possible to progress to a supervisory role should a post become available.

# Forensic computer analyst

Computers are an essential and inescapable part of modern life, both at work and at home. But the growth of digital technologies has led to a corresponding increase in computer-based crime.

The role of the forensic computer analyst is a fairly new development within the forensic world, with computer forensic evidence having been used in criminal trials since the mid-1980s (Casey, 2004). The job entails investigating this type of crime and gathering evidence to help build a case against offenders, whether they are individuals or criminal networks.

Forensic computer analysts are normally employed by companies specialising in forensic computer analysis rather than by police forces, although some of the larger forces (such as the Metropolitan Police Service) do employ forensic computer analysts.

Forensic computer analysts are involved in a range of investigations, such as computer hacking, online scams or fraud. They might investigate political or commercial espionage or theft of sensitive company information by employees. They might track terrorist communications or find the source of illegal pornographic images.

Forensic computer analysts can collect and analyse evidence from computers, even if the evidence has been deleted or corrupted. Evidence can include files, photographs, e-mails and telephone calls. Analysts need to know how to capture evidence without destroying it. They examine items such as computer hard drives and record their findings as possible future evidence. They may have to attend court to give evidence as part of a criminal case.

## Job description

A job description for a forensic computer analyst is given below, to give us an idea of the qualifications, skills and aptitudes required for the role.

## Job purpose

- A forensic computer analyst investigates computer-based crime and assists other law enforcement professionals to investigate and detect this type of crime and prosecute offenders.

## Core work areas

A forensic computer analyst utilises forensic software applications to examine electronic media as diverse as computer hard drives, personal digital assistants or mobile telephones to locate, recover and copy hidden, encrypted or damaged information from such sources.

They can unlock digital images that have been altered to mask the identity of a place or person, analyse mobile phone records to trace devices to a particular location or to rule them out and follow electronic data trails to uncover links between individuals or groups.

Forensic computer analysts must carefully document each stage of their investigation, presenting their technical findings to managers, law enforcement organisations and clients.

Forensic computer analysts must be able to prepare detailed reports and witness statements and attend court to give evidence as necessary (Directgov, 2010).

## Qualifications

A forensic computer analyst will normally be educated to at least honours degree level in computer science or digital forensics. A postgraduate qualification or industry certification may also be a requirement.

## Skills and aptitudes

A forensic computer analyst should ideally have a background in the ICT industry, possibly as a network engineer or developer. They should have knowledge and experience with a number of operating systems such as Windows, Macintosh, Linux or UNIX, and DOS.

A forensic computer analyst must have understanding of information systems security, network architecture, general database concepts, document management, hardware and software troubleshooting, electronic mail systems such as Exchange and GroupWise, Microsoft Office applications, intrusion tools and computer forensic tools such as EnCase, Access Data and FTK. Experience conducting security assessments, penetration testing and ethical hacking is also desirable.

They must be good critical thinkers and problem solvers and have the ability to multitask as a forensic computer analyst would normally be working on more than one investigation at a time. A sense of resilience and the ability to work under pressure and deal with sensitive and distressing images and information is also important.

## Training and development

Computer crime is a very fast moving and dynamic field, and it is extremely important that a forensic computer analyst keeps up to date with the latest developments in criminal methods and investigative techniques. A forensic computer analyst would do this by undertaking further training, such as obtaining postgraduate qualifications, industry certifications and specialised in-house courses.

C  H  A  P  T  E  R          S  U  M  M  A  R  Y

In this chapter, we have looked at the development of forensic services in the United Kingdom, how they have evolved from the first fingerprint bureau opened by the Metropolitan Police Service to the multi-faceted disciplines in use today.

We have looked at some of the main career opportunities, what the jobs entail, what qualifications, skills and attributes a person would need to work in the role and so forth. It should be remembered, however, that the jobs covered in this chapter are not an exhaustive list and only give a flavour of the many opportunities available.

---

CASE STUDY

*On arrival at the scene, one of the first tasks the responding police officers will undertake is to secure the scene to protect any evidence that may be there. They will then request that a CSI attends to examine the scene. The CSI may well be some distance away and may not be able to attend immediately, so it is important that the scene is adequately protected to prevent loss of or damage to evidence.*

*When the CSI attends the scene they are briefed by the investigating officer so that they have an understanding of what has happened (as far as it is known at that time). They also speak to the victim(s) to ascertain a general picture of what has happened – where the suspects stood, what they might have touched and so forth. The CSI then asks to view CCTV footage of the incident, if it is available, as this can be a very useful aid to pinpoint the areas to concentrate on during the examination.*

*The CSI starts the examination by taking a detailed set of photographs. First, they use a wide-angled lens to 'corner' the room. This entails standing in each corner and taking a photograph, ensuring that the photographs 'overlap' so that everything in the room appears in at least one photograph. These photographs provide a valuable record of the scene and can help the investigators check details described in witness statements, and allow jurors at a later trial to put the events being described in context.*

*Next, the CSI takes 'locating' photographs of things deemed to be significant – for instance, a greetings card display that has been knocked over by one of the suspects as they left the shop. The locating photograph shows the item in relation to other parts of the scene, again allowing them to be put in context.*

*The locating photographs are then followed up with close-up views.*

*The CSI makes detailed notes as they examine the scene, including the date and time when the examination started and ended, people present, information given, a sketch plan and a list of any exhibits recovered, with the photographs of the scene listed as the first exhibit.*

*Once the photographs are taken, the CSI starts the 'forensic' section of the investigation, looking for physical evidence such as footwear marks, DNA or fibres left behind by the suspects. It is here that CCTV footage can be really useful, as it directs the CSI to target areas – for instance, the places where the suspects stood can be examined to reveal latent (not easily seen) footwear impressions.*

*The final part of the examination involves looking for fingerprints. Fingerprints can be either visible – in dirt or paint or whatever contaminant the person happens to have on their hands – or latent.*

*Visible impressions can be recovered photographically. This is quite a specialised task, as an actual-sized image needs to be produced for comparison purposes. The photography can also be complicated by the surface the impression is found on – for instance, it may be on a curved surface or on a multicoloured, patterned surface; hence, a photographer with knowledge of advanced photographic techniques may be needed.*

*Latent impressions are formed by the sweat and oils that are naturally present on the hands and transfer onto surfaces that are touched. Latent prints need some form of enhancement to locate them. The most usual technique used is the application of aluminium powder. Aluminium powder consists of small flat flakes of ground aluminium which adhere to the fingerprints and make them visible. The powdered fingerprints can then be 'lifted' off the surface using clear sticky tape and secured onto a sheet of acetate for transport to the fingerprint bureau.*

*Aluminium powder works well on clean, smooth, shiny surfaces, but not so well on textured surfaces such as plastics, paper or cardboard. Luckily there are many different chemicals that can be utilised to show up fingerprints on surfaces unsuitable for treatment with aluminium powder, so if fingerprinting of such an item is required, the CSI can call on the services of the chemical enhancement technician.*

*At this particular scene, the CSI recovered the following.*

### Footwear impressions
*The impressions recovered were from two different types of shoe and could well have been left by the two suspects. Footwear impressions are a valuable evidence type as they can be conclusively linked to the shoes that made them. However, these links can only be established once the shoes have been recovered and so do not initially help to identify offenders.*

### Fibres
*A small clump of fibres were found adhering to the greetings card display rack that was knocked over by one of the suspects. These fibres may well have come from the suspect's clothing. If the item of clothing was recovered and a match established between the fibres making up the garment and those found at the crime scene, this would provide supporting evidence that the suspect had been at the scene.*

### Fingerprints
*The CCTV footage showed that as they left the shop, one of the suspects tripped, knocking over a greetings card display rack that was near the door. The suspect stopped himself from falling by steadying himself against a glass display case. When the display case was examined using aluminium powder, latent fingerprints were revealed.*

*Moreover, the CSI recovered some greetings cards that the suspect may have touched, so that they could be examined by the chemical enhancement technician.*

After completing their examination of the scene, the CSI takes fingerprints from the staff in the shop, so that any fingerprints lifted at the scene that belong to the staff can be quickly eliminated, allowing the fingerprint officer to concentrate on those fingerprints most likely to have been left by the suspects.

The fingerprints recovered by the CSI are immediately taken to the fingerprint bureau, where a fingerprint officer will attempt to identify the suspects by comparing the fingerprints found at the scene with those held on the fingerprint database.

Of the evidence recovered by the CSI, the fingerprints are potentially the most useful to the initial investigation because a successful identification would give the investigators the name of their suspects at an early stage in the investigation.

## Self-assessment questions

1. Who were the first forensic scientists?

2. Whose 'exchange principle' is the basis for forensic investigation?

3. Which piece of legislation led to crime scene staff being designated as investigators?

4. What are the two grades of a fingerprint officer?

5. How long does it take to become a fingerprint expert?

6. What does the acronym FERRT stand for?

7. What previous experience might be helpful to the role of a chemical enhancement technician?

8. What qualifications would help you to get a job as a police photographer?

9. As a police photographer, what types of photography should you be proficient in?

10. What is the minimum qualification normally required to work as a forensic computer analyst?

*REFERENCES*

Association of Chief Police Officers/Forensic Science Service (ACPO/FSS) (1996) *Using Forensic Science Effectively*. Birmingham: ACPO/FSS.

Beavan, C (2003) *Fingerprints*. London: Fourth Estate.

Casey, E (2004) *Digital Evidence and Computer Crime*, 2nd edition. London: Academic Press.

Directgov (2010) *Forensic Computer Analyst*. Available online at https://nextstep.direct.gov.uk/PlanningYourCareer/JobProfiles/JobProfile1496/Pages/default.aspx (accessed 3 April 2011).

Great Britain Parliament (2002) *The Police Reform Act*. London: The Stationery Office.

Henry, E R (1934) *Classification and Uses of Fingerprints*, 7th edition. London: HMSO.

LGC Forensics (2011) *LGC Forensics*. Available online at www.lgc.co.uk/divisions/lgc_forensics.aspx (accessed 22 March 2011).

McCartney, C (2006) *Forensic Identification and Criminal Justice, Forensic Science, Justice and Risk*. Cullompton: Willan.

National Policing Improvement Agency (NPIA) (2010a) *Fingerprint Training*. Available online at www.npia.police.uk/en/6396.htm (accessed 31 March 2011).

National Policing Improvement Agency (NPIA) (2010b) *Fingerprint Evidence Recording and Retrieval (FERRT)*. Available online at www.npia.police.uk/en/1486.htm (accessed 3 April 2011).

Nickell, J and Fischer, J F (1999) Crime Science Methods of Forensic Detection. *Encyclopaedia of Forensic Science*. San Diego: Academic Press.

O' Neill, E (2006) *Mark of Innocence, The Guardian*. Available online at www.guardian.co.uk/uk/2006/apr/18/ukcrime.features11 (accessed 2 April 2011).

Pepper, I K (2010) *Crime Scene Investigation Methods and Procedures*, 2nd edition. Maidenhead: Open University Press.

Siegel, J A, Saukko, P J and Knupfer, G C (2000) *Encyclopaedia of Forensic Science*. San Diego: Academic Press.

Skillset: the sector skills council for creative media (2009) *Forensic Photographer Job Profile*. Available online at www.skillset.org/photo/careers/photographers/article_3424_1.asp (accessed 3 April 2011).

Sutton, R and Trueman, K (eds) (2009) *Crime Scene Management Scene Specific Methods*. Oxford: Wiley.

Touche Ross (1987) *Review of Scientific Support for the Police*, volume 3. London: Home Office.

Warlen, S C (1995) Crime Scene Photography: The Silent Witness. *Journal of Forensic Identification*, 45(3): 261–5.

# 4    The investigation evolves

BARRIE SHELDON

## CHAPTER OBJECTIVES

By the end of this chapter you will have:

- gained a knowledge and understanding of the history and development of criminal investigation within the police service;
- gained a knowledge and understanding of the investigative role, the skills required, and the selection and training attributed to the role;
- considered and analysed some of the issues and challenges that face a modern investigator.

## Introduction

This chapter primarily explores the history and functions of those leading the investigation.

- Police detective (constable).
- Police staff investigator (civilian).

The chapter considers the recruitment, selection, assessment and training for a police detective (constable) and a police staff investigator (civilian). Their role and function within the investigative process is explored as also how they could be utilised as part of the team responsible for the investigation of a robbery such as the one at Roman's Newsagents in High Street.

Before examining the two roles, it is important that they are considered in context by exploring the historical development of criminal investigation. The use of plain clothes police officers commonly referred to as 'detectives' has been problematic in the past, and the police service has received much criticism about its ability to effectively investigate crime.

However, this should be considered in perspective. The police service has a long and much respected tradition with the majority of staff working honestly and diligently and achieving much success; however, evidence shows that corruption has brought the police service into disrepute, and a series of detrimental high-profile cases has questioned their investigative capability.

A brief journey through relevant police history will not only provide an overview of some of the problems the police service has had to face but also show how, today, the police service is more professional, has robust investigative processes in place and is supported by staff who have the skills to meet the modern demands of criminal investigation.

# Criminal investigation – historical perspectives

## Nineteenth century

During the early years of the modern police service, the public had little confidence in the ability of the police to detect crime and prosecute offenders. The main focus of the Metropolitan Police was in preventive policing and they had no effective detection strategy. The use of plain clothes officers to assist with crime detection was limited owing to certain political tensions, including the potential of the police being accused of being 'government spies' and also encouraging the commission of certain offences as an 'agent provocateur' (Rawlings, 2002, p 168).

The Metropolitan Police introduced its first detective division in 1842, and the number of detectives slowly increased. In 1869, its central detective capability was increased and 180 divisional detectives were appointed to undertake surveillance of known criminals (Rawlings, 2002, page 174). Failure to detect a number of high-profile murder cases and a corruption scandal that involved senior detectives resulted in the detective division being disbanded, and in 1878 the first Criminal Investigation Department (CID) was established, led by Howard Vincent.

Despite the introduction of the CID, the public was critical of the ability of the police to effectively investigate crime. The 1880s saw the police using techniques of entrapment and failing to solve more high-profile murders, including those in Whitechapel believed to be the work of the infamous 'Jack the Ripper', between 1887 and 1889. The Irish Fenian bombing campaign in London also contributed to a lack of confidence in the police. In essence, detectives were failing to deliver, their operating methods were secretive, they bargained for information without any control and they ignored minor breaches of the law (Rawlings, 2002, p 176).

## Twentieth century

The debate regarding policing and its effectiveness continued, but it was the latter part of the twentieth century which saw real controversy, scandal and justified criticism of the police service, particularly in the effectiveness and integrity of its investigative practices.

*The nadir (lowest point) of police legitimacy was reached at the start of the final decade of the twentieth century, as indicated by many indices of public and police opinion.*

(Reiner, 2000, p 47)

Police corruption in particular had become a big issue and in a report in *The Times*, 1969 allegations were made against detectives that included the covering up of serious crimes, setting up criminals as agent provocateurs, perjury and planting evidence. The paper reported a systematic, institutionalised and widespread network of corruption (Reiner, 2000, p 62).

Subsequent Metropolitan Police Commissioners, Sir Robert Mark and Sir David McNee, took positive action to tackle the problems of corruption which included the disbanding of certain specialist squads such as drugs and obscene publications, and new policies were introduced to exert more control over the detectives.

### Miscarriages of justice

In addition to the adverse publicity about corrupt practices, other events started to unfold that questioned the police's ability to effectively investigate crime. Police powers were governed by common law, statute and most controversially the 'Judges' Rules' that were introduced in 1912 providing the police with judicial guidance for the detention and questioning of suspects. These rules could easily be flouted, and following a series of miscarriages of justice, they were brought into disrepute.

In 1972, three youths were arrested for the murder of Maxwell Confait in Lewisham, London. The youths were aged 14, 15 (with a very low IQ) and 18 years (with a mental age of 8). All were interviewed without an adult being present and at the later trial claimed that confessions were only made because of police brutality. All were convicted, but following a long campaign, the case went to the Court of Appeal in 1975 which overturned the convictions and the three were released from prison. In November of the same year, the government announced an enquiry into the investigation and appointed Sir Henry Fisher as chair who published his report in December 1977. Sir Henry suggested that a Royal Commission be set up to look at the issue of police investigations, and the following year a Royal Commission on Criminal Procedure (RCCP) was announced by government.

The RCCP reported in 1981 and recommended an overhaul of the criminal investigative process. It highlighted the need to maintain a balance between powers and duties of the police and rights and duties of suspects. The Police and Criminal Evidence (PACE) Act, 1984, introduced in January 1986 provided a statutory framework for the criminal investigation process. The Judges' Rules were abolished, and PACE Codes of practice were published that clearly stated the rights of an individual and powers of the police for certain key areas of police procedure. There are currently eight codes of practice:

1. Code A: Stop and search.

2. Code B: Searching of premises and seizure of property.

3. Code C: Detention treatment and questioning.

4. Code D: Identification.

5. Code E: Audio recording of interviews with suspects.

6. Code F: Visual recording of interviews.

7. Code G: Power of arrest.

8. Code H: Detention, questioning and treatment of terrorist suspects.

---

### REFLECTIVE TASK

*PACE Act and associated PACE Codes of Practice provide the core framework of police powers and safeguards around stop and search, arrest, detention, investigation, identification and interviewing detainees (Home Office, 2010). Reflect on the implications of this act of Parliament and how it was designed to control the police service.*

---

Despite the introduction of PACE which exerted more control over the investigative process and afforded suspects more protection, a series of miscarriages of justice and other events further rocked the public's confidence in the police. Table 4.1 provides a timeline of some of the key events that contributed to public concerns.

The miscarriages of justice highlighted significant problems with the criminal justice system (CJS). The police were being seen as confession orientated in their investigative approach and willing to turn to questionable means to obtain confessions (Savage, 2007, page 41). Despite PACE 1984 that introduced safeguards for those detained and interviewed in police custody, there was clear evidence that the legislation and associated codes of practice were still open to abuse and did not provide as much control of police powers as originally envisaged.

### 1993 Royal Commission
On the same day the Birmingham six (Table 4.1) were acquitted, the government announced a further Royal Commission to review the CJS in England and Wales. The commission's brief was to examine the effectiveness of the CJS in securing the conviction of those who were guilty of offences and ensuring that the innocent were acquitted (Savage, 2007). Specific terms of reference included reviewing the conduct and control of police investigations and their supervision.

The RCCP made a number of key recommendations that resulted in new legislation. The Criminal Justice and Public Order Act 1994 allowed inferences to be drawn in certain circumstances when a suspect chose to remain silent

*Table 4.1 Events leading to the introduction of PACE*

| Year | Event | Allegations of police malpractice |
|---|---|---|
| 1989 | Four men (Guilford four) convicted in 1975 for bombings in Guilford and Woolwich. Convictions quashed by the Court of Appeal | Flaws in the way Surrey detectives noted down confessions. Notes not written at the time and evidence of detectives colluding in writing up of notes |
| 1989 | West Midlands Serious Crime Squad was disbanded following a series of complaints and revelations of malpractice in court trials. Over 30 convictions were subsequently quashed by the Court of Appeal | Fabricated confessions and allegations of torture such as putting a plastic bag over suspect's head |
| 1991 | Six men (Birmingham six) convicted in 1974 for two bombings in the city centre that killed 21 people. Convictions quashed by the Court of Appeal | Men claimed they had been beaten up to make confessions. Scientific tests also showed that confession statements had been altered at a later date |
| 1991 | Winston Silcott and two others convicted of the murder of Police Constable Keith Blakelock in 1985 during riots in Tottenham, London. Conviction quashed by the Court of Appeal | Silcott deprived of rights and scientific tests proved that parts of the written confession had been fabricated |
| 1992 | Judith Ward convicted in 1974 for the killing of 12 people who died when their coach was bombed on the M62 motorway. Conviction quashed by the Court of Appeal | History of mental illness not mentioned at trial. Changed confession several times and prosecution only selected parts of statements made by the accused to suit their case |
| 1992 | Stefan Kiszko convicted in 1976 for the murder of Lesley Molseed, 11 years. Conviction quashed by the Court of Appeal | Vulnerable suspect with a physical condition that would have made it impossible for him to have committed the crime |
| 1997 | Four men convicted in 1979 of the murder of a Carl Bridgewater, 13 years. Released from prison after Court of Appeal ruled that the conviction was unsafe | One of the four, Patrick Molloy, who died in prison in 1981, claimed that he was purposely deprived of sleep and that salt was put in his food. Scientific tests also showed that alterations had been made to a written confession |

(sections 34–39) and provided the police with extra powers to obtain intimate and non-intimate samples for DNA analysis and extend the retention parameters for the DNA database (sections 54–59). The Criminal Procedure and Investigations Act 1996 introduced the concept of 'disclosure' that requires the prosecution to disclose all material collected during an investigation to the accused (section 3). The act also requires the accused to disclose a defence statement to the court and prosecution prior to trial (section 5[5]). The rules of disclosure provided new challenges for the police service with investigators being required to undergo disclosure training, and in more complex cases such as major investigations, a new role, the 'disclosure officer' was introduced.

The RCCP recommendations also resulted in the Criminal Appeals Act 1995 that paved the way for the introduction of the Criminal Defence Review Commission in 1997 responsible for the review of possible miscarriages of justice and to decide whether they should be referred to an appeal court.

### Investigative interviewing

The miscarriages of justice had also clearly identified a problem with police investigative interviewing. The confession-orientated approach was problematic, and research revealed that generally police officers were poor at interviewing. Research revealed that police interviewers failed to prepare properly, were inept and used poor techniques, assumed guilt of the suspect, failed to establish relevant facts and exerted too much pressure (Baldwin, 1992, p 14).

There was a clear need to move towards a more ethical approach to interviewing with a goal of searching for the truth rather than seeking a confession at all costs. Seven principles of investigative interviewing were introduced by the government (Home Office Circular 22/92), which provided the foundation for a standardised framework of ethical interviewing that the police service adopted. The model used is referred to as PEACE which is a mnemonic for the stages of the interview process: planning and preparation, engage and explain, account, closure and evaluation.

PEACE training was delivered to all police officers responsible for interviewing victims, witnesses and suspects, and the skills required for this key task were important considerations for those responsible for recruitment, selection and training at all levels within the police service.

The training, delivery and application of the PEACE model of investigative interviewing was not without its problems and resulted in a number of changes. In 2004 a new system of training was adopted that introduced five tiers of investigative-interview training that provided training commensurate to the role of the officer concerned. It also considered the experience, skills and previous training of each officer and the complexity of the interviews required (Shawyer et al., 2009, p 34).

### Stephen Lawrence

In Chapter 2, aspects of the 1999 Sir William Macpherson report into the murder of Stephen Lawrence in 1993 was discussed in respect of race and diversity (p 27). The report also highlighted the incompetency of the police investigation particularly during the early stages where key decisions and actions were not taken that contributed to a failed investigation. The perpetrators of this crime have still not been brought to justice.

*The conclusions to be drawn from all the evidence in connection with the investigation of Stephen Lawrence's racist murder are clear. There is no doubt but that there were fundamental errors. The investigation was marred by a combination of professional incompetence, institutional racism and a failure of leadership by senior officers. A flawed MPS review failed to expose these inadequacies. The second investigation could not salvage the faults of the first investigation.*

(Macpherson, 1999, p 46.1)

By the time the report had been published, the police service had already taken a number of steps to improve their investigative processes and procedures particularly in the discipline of major investigations.

### Major investigations

A high-profile, well-publicised serial murder investigation highlighted further evidence of the limitations of police investigation. The case was that of Peter Sutcliffe (nicknamed the Yorkshire ripper), who was convicted at the Central Criminal Court in London on 22 May 1981 for 13 cases of murder and seven cases of attempted murder.

The government immediately commissioned a review of the police investigations led by Lawrence Byford (Her Majesty's Inspector of Constabulary), who made a number of recommendations that included the standardisation of documents and procedures, computerisation of records and the selection and training of staff (Byford, 1981, pages 153–5).

As a result, Major Incident Room Standardised Administrative Procedures (MIRSAP) was introduced nationally, that established protocols for the handling, use and storage of information collected by the police during a major investigation. In 1986 a Home Office Large Major Enquiry System (HOLMES) was introduced to the police service and since this time its functionality has been developed further. It now provides a sophisticated management system for major investigations, adopted and used by a range of law enforcement agencies throughout the United Kingdom.

---

REFLECTIVE TASK

*Consider the implications of these events and subsequent changes to legislation from a police recruitment, selection and training perspective. What are the potential economic and resource issues, and what is the impact on police structures and staffing profiles, for example, the police officer and police staff mix?*

---

## Twenty-first century

The Labour government following their electoral success in 1997 introduced a radical programme of change for the CJS which was delivered throughout the first decade of the twenty-first century. The initial plans were set out in 2001 in a government White Paper 'Policing a New Century: A Blueprint for Reform' which contained a range of proposed actions to reform the police service. The home secretary, David Blunkett, in his foreword stated:

> *... we want to look at the way in which we can substantially improve the standard, reliability, consistency, and responsiveness of the service.*
>
> (Home Office, 2001)

Among the plethora of new innovations and directions set out by the government was the introduction of two new police bodies: a Police Standards Unit (PSU) and a National Centre of Policing Excellence (NCPE). Both had an important role to play in the development and reform of policing. It was the role of the PSU to identify and disseminate good practice in order to deliver a national consistency in the prevention and detection of crime, the arrest and prosecution of offenders and the delivery of services to the public and victims of crime. The NCPE was seen as a centre of excellence for all aspects of operational policing, promoting professionally validated, evidence-based practices (Home Office, 2001, pages 41 and 129). In essence, the government was making positive moves to professionalise the police service and seeking to standardise police practice and procedure.

The NCPE was replaced by the National Police Improvement Agency (NPIA) in 2005, but during their tenure, they developed a series of doctrines to improve policing standards nationally. Two key doctrines were developed by the NCPE. The first was concerned with intelligence-led policing and the national intelligence model now established as a national standard framework not only for the police service but also for other law enforcement agencies. Second, they introduced an investigative doctrine in 2005 – 'Practice Advice on Core Investigative Doctrine'.

The core investigative doctrine provides a strategic overview of the investigative process and guidance to all investigators on the key principles of criminal investigation. It provides a framework of good practice:

> *Its purpose is to provide investigators with the skills and knowledge they require to conduct investigations in a competent manner, inspiring confidence in the investigator and the wider criminal justice system.*
>
> (Association of Chief Police Officers, 2005, p 7)

This is a key document for any criminal investigator, and any selection process and training programme will be based on this doctrine.

---

**PRACTICAL TASK**

*Obtain a copy of the 'Practice Advice on Core Investigative Doctrine 2005' that can be found online at www.ssiacymru.org.uk/media/pdf/6/c/Core_Investigation_ Doctrine_Interactive_1_.pdf and read the introductory section. Find out how a criminal investigation is defined, the role of an investigator, the benefits of an investigation and the purpose of the core investigative doctrine.*

*This is a key document for any investigator and will be useful both for preparing to undertake an investigator's role and for guidance as an investigative practitioner.*

### National investigative training

In Chapter 3, the Initial Police Learning and Development Programme (IPLDP) and how national occupational standards for policing and law enforcement were introduced by Skills for Justice within an integrated competency framework (ICF) were explained. Similarly, the Association of Chief Police Officers (ACPO) in conjunction with NCPE was commissioned by the Home Office to examine, develop and make recommendations to professionalise criminal investigations.

### Professionalising the investigative process (PIP)

PIP was the result of the ACPO and NCPE collaboration and is now embedded as the national standard across the police service. The programme aims to make the criminal investigation process more professional, ethical and effective through the use of training, mentors and the development of accredited investigators. PIP is aligned to the same policing professional framework as IPLDP and provides a pathway for both the career detective seeking opportunities for promotion and the continual professional development of investigators seeking to develop their skills.

PIP is divided into three levels and provides a training regime tailored to meet the needs of investigators at all levels.

Level 1

- IPLDP – all student police officers.

- Modular stand-alone course to meet specific training needs such as police officers employed by the police service prior to the introduction of PIP.

- Specialist – family liaison officer (road death).

- Specialist – sexual offence investigator.

- Investigative interviewing for volume and priority investigations.

Level 2

- Initial Crime Investigators Development Programme (ICIDP).

- Initial management of serious crime.

- Detective inspector's development programme.

- Specialist – child abuse investigator.

- Specialist – family liaison officer (major crime or mass fatality).

- Investigative interviewing for serious and complex investigations.
- Managing and co-ordinating interviews for complex or major investigations (interview advisor).

Level 3

- Senior investigating officer development programme.

The descriptions given in the following table detail the national occupational standards attributed to the three levels.

*Table 4.2 National Occupational Standards by level*

| PIP levels of competency | NOS unit reference |
| --- | --- |
| *Level 1* | |
| Conduct priority and volume investigations | CI 101 |
| Interview victims and witnesses in relation to priority and volume investigations | CJ 101 |
| Interview suspects in relation to priority and volume investigations | CJ 201 |
| *Level 2* | |
| Conduct serious and complex investigations | CI 102 |
| Interview victims and witnesses in relation to serious and complex investigations | CJ 102 |
| Interview suspects in relation to serious and complex investigations | CJ 202 |
| Specialist — carry out specialist interviews with victims and witnesses | CJ 103 |
| Specialist – carry out specialist interviews with suspects | CJ 203 |
| Interview co-ordinator – manage and co-ordinate interviews for serious, complex or major investigations | CJ 301 |
| *Level 3* | |
| Manage major investigations | CI 103 |

(NPIA, 2010a)

PIP is a key training programme for the police service and continues to be developed. For the purposes of this chapter, the focus will be at level 2 and the ICIDP which is the prime training programme for those police officers who wish to become investigators and achieve the status of detective constable (DC).

> PRACTICAL TASK
>
> *Before reading the next section, consider the role of a police detective today and write down a list of responsibilities you think a detective has.*
>
> *You will note that some of these responsibilities overlap with that of the patrol officer (see Chapter 2). Where overlaps exist, identify any differences in the detective role.*

*Now write down a list of skills that you think may be required by a detective to effectively carry out the role. For example, a person who is suspected of committing a criminal offence will need to be questioned so a detective will require good interviewing skills.*

# Role of the detective

The role of a detective in the twenty-first century is diverse and complex, and demands a high level of skill. The structure of police organisations post–World War II was relatively simple with four main branches of work based around incident response, community policing, road traffic and criminal investigation. Criminal investigation locally was in the first instance dealt with by uniformed response and community officers, who were mainly responsible for low-level (volume crime) investigations such as theft, assault, vehicle crime and criminal damage. The more complex and protracted criminal investigations would be referred to the CID which was made up of plain clothed police officers. Their work mainly consisted of investigation, evidence collection and case preparation. When a particular crime became a problem, such as a spate of house burglaries or theft from motor vehicles, ad hoc squads would be set up in an attempt to alleviate the problem.

In addition to local provision, there would be central support (police headquarters) which would provide a cadre of specialists to assist with crime investigations such as murder investigation, and specialist, covert and forensic services. Nationally, more crime investigation support was available through regional crime squads and later the national crime squad, replaced by the Serious and Organised Police Agency (SOCA) in 2006. In July 2010, Theresa May, home secretary, announced that SOCA would be replaced by a National Crime Agency.

The modern era has seen significant changes to police organisational structures brought about by a series of social, economic and political factors. The problems of corruption and the miscarriages of justice have already been discussed earlier, but other factors such as legislative change, and an increasing demand for policing services has resulted in the re-organisation and re-structuring of police departments.

# The detective constable

A DC requires a good range of investigative skills, and the ICF provides a set of core responsibilities and behaviours for the role. In the previous task, you completed a list of skills that can be compared with the core responsibilities and behaviours (as set out below). They are used for recruitment, selection and assessment purposes, and each one will be briefly discussed.

## Core responsibilities

- Investigation.
- Intelligence.
- Custody and prosecution.
- Police operations.
- Personal responsibility.
- Health, safety and welfare.
- Community safety.

## Behaviours

- Leading people.
- Leading the organisation.
- Leading the way.
- Personal qualities and values.

## Investigation

Activity within this section includes:

- the interviewing of victims, witnesses and suspects;
- care for victims and witnesses;
- crime scene preservation;
- searching persons, vehicles, premises and land.

The detective has a responsibility to ensure that the investigation is completed both expeditiously and thoroughly in accordance with policy and legislative requirements.

## Intelligence

In any investigation, intelligence can play an important role in identifying potential suspects. Activities are centred round the gathering and use of intelligence to support crime and disorder objectives and to ensure that it is gathered and used ethically in accordance with relevant legislation, policy, protocols and codes of practice. The recruitment of covert human intelligence sources (informants) and the use of surveillance techniques and associated equipment, regulated by the Regulation of Investigatory Powers Act 2000, play an important part in the investigative process. A detective will need to know legislative restrictions and requirements adhere to local policy and procedures and how to operate surveil-lance equipment.

## Custody and prosecution

In most cases when a suspect is identified for a crime, an arrest is made and the suspect is detained at a police station. A detective requires good knowledge and understanding of both arrest and custody procedures applied in accordance with codes of practice and legislative requirements. Human rights, security, and health and safety issues also need to be considered and applied accordingly.

Once a suspect has been interviewed and charged with an offence, a detective is responsible for preparing and presenting a case file for the prosecution, and when required attend a court or other hearing to give evidence.

## Police operations

There are many types of police operation, for example, a raid on premises used for drugs or prostitution, the planned targeting of prolific criminals or even organis-ing a number of arrests following a series of house burglaries. A detective will be required to:

- effectively plan, prepare for and participate in police operations;
- consider operational threats and risks;
- ensure that the operation is both ethical and conforms to the best practice.

## Personal responsibility

Personal responsibility incorporates a wide range of activities that includes:

- completion of administration procedures;
- compliance with health and safety legislation;
- maintaining standards of professional practice;
- making the best use of technology;
- promoting equality, diversity and human rights within working practices;
- providing an organisational response that recognises the needs of the community;
- working as part of a team.

## Health, safety and welfare

This relates directly to first aid and requires the ability to identify the nature of an illness or injury and provide necessary first-aid treatment in accordance with approved procedures. You may ask why this particular activity has been included within the role profile and its relevance. First aid was identified as an issue to be addressed within the Stephen Lawrence report, and three recommendations were made including the following:

> *That First Aid training for all 'public contact' police officers (including senior officers) should at once be reviewed and revised to ensure that they have basic skills to apply First Aid. Officers must be taught to 'think first aid', and first and foremost 'A (Airways), B (Breathing) and C (Circulation)'.*
>
> (Macpherson, 1999, recommendation 45)

## Community safety

This activity simply relates to the safe driving of a police vehicle, having consideration for others in accordance with policy and in line with the system of car control.

## Leading people

A detective is part of a team and as an effective team member is expected to help build relationships, and actively help and support others to achieve team goals. They should also be able to communicate ideas and information effectively, both verbally and in writing, using a language and communication style appropriate to the audience.

## Leading the organisation

A detective is required to have good planning skills, be well organised and to demonstrate evidence of being able to solve problems and make sound decisions. They should be able to provide a community and customer focus, provide a high level of service to customers and meet their needs. Victims and witnesses are prime examples of a customer.

## Leading the way

A detective is required to demonstrate respect for race and diversity by understanding the views of others, being tactful and diplomatic, and treating people with dignity and respect. They are able to understand and are sensitive to social, cultural and racial differences and respect opinions, circumstances and feelings of colleagues and members of the public no matter what their race, religion, position, background, circumstances, status or appearance.

## Personal qualities and values

Achieving results is important for any organisation and the police service is no exception. Good results reflect well on the individual, the team and the organisation and enhance public confidence in the police to reduce and detect crime. A detective has responsibility for their own actions, should be able to sort out problems as they arise, should achieve results to the required standards and should take responsibility for their own personal development.

# Selection

To attain the role of a detective, certain skills and prerequisites are required. These can vary from one police force to another, and even within the same police force may vary across Basic Command Units (BCUs), sometimes referred to as 'divisions'. An example from West Mercia Police (Shropshire 'F' Division) is given below.

- Completion of the IPLDP.

- Satisfactory performance within the workplace evidenced through a personal development review (PDR) process.

- Recommendation or endorsement from a supervisor to verify that the applicant is suitable for the role.

- Three-month attachment to the CID as a temporary DC.

- Subject to a successful attachment, then put on list to fill detective vacancies.

- Where list exceeds vacancies, a selection process is conducted. The selection is by way of a competitive interview with candidates assessed against skill competencies. Based on the performance within the interview, the candidate will be scored, and those with highest scores are selected.

- Upon appointment as a DC, further training is provided.

(Humphreys, 2010)

# Training and assessment

Having been selected for a detective post, a police officer will be required to complete the ICIDP (PIP level 2 – page 75). The programme consists of three phases:

*Phase 1*: Completion of a national investigator's multiple-choice examination that tests knowledge of law and procedure relevant to the role of a trainee investigator. The examination consists of 80 questions, over two hours, and progression to phases 1 and 2 of the ICIDP is dependent on achieving a pass mark.

*Phase 2*: A six-week full-time study course.

*Phase 3*: Attaining national occupational standards within the workplace.

(NPIA, 2010b)

*Find out about the rules and the syllabus for the national investigator's examination that can be accessed via the following Internet link: www.npia.police.uk/ en/16453.htm.*

*Some sections of the police service now work with Higher Education providers to further enhance investigative knowledge and skills. For example, Cheshire Police now deliver their ICIDP in conjunction with Chester University and Cleveland Police with Teesside University. Upon completion of the programme, a detective is awarded with a diploma in criminal investigation.*

# Police staff investigator

Social, economic and political factors have seen the police service shift to a more business-orientated organisation, working to performance targets (reduced to one central target, 2010), striving to achieve 'best value', accredit services and processes, and professionalise staff. During the past 20 years, the police service has increased its police staff portfolio in an attempt to remove police officers from administrative roles and others where police powers are not required. For example, scenes-of-crime officers used to be mainly police officers but now most are police staff. Further, section 38(2) Police Reform Act 2002 allowed a chief officer of police to employ and designate powers to police staff. The act provided for community support officers, investigating officers, detention officers and escort officers. Table 4.3 compiled from various Home Office statistics demonstrates how police staff numbers have increased since 1997.

Police staff are now an integral part of investigation teams nationally and can be found in many departments responsible for criminal investigation. The management and investigation of crime is complex, and sophisticated structures are in place to respond effectively to the challenge of combating crime within the constraints of legislative requirements and government targets. An example of crime structures within a county police force (Staffordshire Police, 2009a,b) is given in

*Table 4.3 Police service strength 1997–2010*

| Police service strength | 1997 | 2000 | 2005 | 2010 |
|---|---|---|---|---|
| Police officers | 1,27,158 | 1,21,779 | 1,42,795 | 1,43,734 |
| Police staff | 56,651 | 56,738 | 74,417 | 83,845 |
| Special constables | 19,874 | 13,528 | 11,918 | 15,505 |
| Community support officers | 0 | 0 | 6,214 | 16,918 |
| Totals | 2,03,683 | 1,92,045 | 2,35,344 | 2,60,002 |

Source: Research Development Statistics (2010)

*Table 4.4 Functions of each department*

| Public protection | Intelligence | Level 2 operations |
|---|---|---|
| Child protection; sex offender management; dangerous offender management; witness protection; criminal records bureau; firearms/explosives licensing; crime reduction | Force intelligence bureau: Central authorities; regional intelligence; covert intelligence; crime stoppers; senior analyst; prison intelligence | Special branch; autocrime; major crime unit; surveillance team; covert operations team; technicians; commercial fraud; financial investigation |
| **Principal SIO** | **Forensic identification** | **Operations (uniformed specialists)** |
| Cadre of senior investigating officers. Major incident room team: office manager; receiver; indexer; action allocator; exhibits officer; disclosure officer; investigators; family liaison officer; crime analyst; researcher | Scenes-of-crime officers for both major crime and volume crime; fingerprint bureau; photography; central forensic submissions; audio visual; hi-tech crime | Tactical support group; roads policing; collision investigation; tactical planning; firearms officers; dog handlers |

Adapted from Staffordshire Police (2009a).

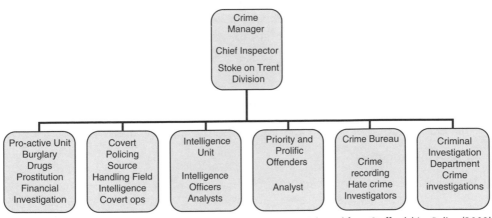

Adapted from Staffordshire Police (2009b)

Table 4.4. It has a 'Protective Services' division at police headquarters providing central support throughout the county to four territorial divisions (BCUs). Each BCU has a crime manager who is responsible for a number of crime departments and teams (Figure 4.1).

Within most of the departments and units highlighted in Table 4.4, there will be a mix of police officers and police staff.

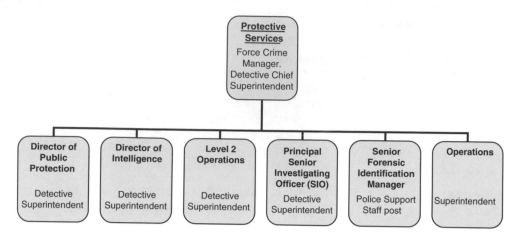

- Refers to National Intelligence Model crime classification – cross-border issues affecting more than one BCU within a force or affecting another force or regional crime activity and usually requiring additional resources

*Figure 4.1  Protective services division*

# Investigator's role

Defining an investigator's role for police staff within the police service is not a simple task because there are many different types of investigator working within a diverse range of police departments and units. For example, within the ICF, there are six separate investigative role profiles for police staff employed within counter terrorism units.

1. CCTV officer.

2. Communications investigations officer.

3. Financial investigator.

4. Hi-tech investigator.

5. Major incident room investigation officer.

6. Special prosecutions investigator.

(Skills for Justice, 2009)

Another example is a police major incident room typically used for murder or other serious crime investigations. It is made up of a mix of police officers and police staff undertaking various investigation roles such as exhibits officer, disclosure officer or support investigator. Table 4.5 below provides a list of 'principal accountabilities' for a support investigation officer within the Nottinghamshire Police Homicide Unit and gives us some insight into what an investigator does within the police organisation.

Within a BCU, police staff investigator roles can be found in various guises such as being employed as part of an interview team, taking statements, file preparation or CCTV investigation.

*Table 4.5 Principal accountabilities for a support investigation officer*

| | |
|---|---|
| 1 | Conduct interviews with witnesses and obtain statements from them to a high standard |
| 2 | Undertake allocated tasks and activities identified as being necessary in support of a criminal investigation. Carry out such tasks in an efficient and effective manner ensuring the seizure, preservation and integrity of relevant documentary and other evidence in accordance with legislative requirements and Force policies and procedures. Gather, analyse and create intelligence utilising appropriate intelligence systems as required by the National Intelligence Model process |
| 3 | Complete reports, letters, memoranda, prosecution files and other relevant paperwork in a concise, accurate and timely manner |
| 4 | Assist investigating officers in planning and preparing interviews with suspects of criminal offences in accordance with the Police and Criminal Evidence Act 1984 |
| 5 | Maintain contact and visits to witnesses who have made statements, particularly vulnerable witnesses who may become protected witnesses. |
| 6 | Where required, attend court to give evidence as a witness or to support the investigation as directed by the senior investigating officer (SIO) |
| 7 | Attend briefings and case conferences as required by the SIO and impart relevant information in order to assist the investigation or particular prosecution case |
| 8 | Perform the role of exhibits officer taking responsibility for the receipt and handling of all exhibits coming into possession of a particular enquiry team. Ensure their integrity, continuity and appropriate storage and subsequent submission for forensic examination in line with the SIO's instructions. Attend post-mortem examinations to perform this role as directed by the SIO |
| 9 | Maintain personal responsibility for gathering, recording, storing, accessing and sharing information in compliance with the information security policy |
| 10 | Perform the role of disclosure officer taking responsibility for the classification of material relevant to a particular investigation in line with the Criminal Procedure and Investigations Act 1996 |
| 11 | To participate in the Force PDR process and take responsibility for identifying your own professional and career development needs |

(Nottinghamshire Police, 2008)

# Selection and training

Police staff can be recruited for an investigator's role both internally and externally. Typical recruiting processes include scrutiny of written applications (paper-sift) to ensure that applicants have the necessary qualifications, experience and prerequisites for the role. The applicant would then be invited to attend an interview or assessment centre where suitability for the role is tested.

Some investigative roles can be restricted to the general public. For example, where statement takers or interviewers are required, some police employers may prefer to recruit retired police officers who are already trained and have the necessary skills and experience. A section of a role profile for an investigator that is quite explicit about the knowledge and experience required for the role is provided below:

- A thorough knowledge of relevant criminal law including the PACE Act 1984.
- Experience of interviewing suspects and witnesses.
- Experience of investigating serious crime.

(West Mercia Police, 2010)

Not all police staff investigator roles are restricted in this way, and in many cases, once an applicant for a post has been successful, appropriate training is provided. For example, an investigator within a Major Investigation Team may be provided with HOLMES 2 training.

Police staff investigators generally tend to have more of a supportive investigative role rather than being responsible for an investigation from start to finish. They are not aligned to PIP; however, being in the midst of an economic recession with the police service facing major financial cuts, the use of police staff investigators is likely to increase.

## C H A P T E R   S U M M A R Y

The chapter has provided a brief historical perspective of the development of criminal investigation within the police service. Problems relating to police corruption, poor performance and miscarriages of justice have highlighted past limitations of the ability of the police service to effectively investigate crime. However, great strides have been taken during the latter part of the twentieth century and twenty-first century to professionalise the investigative process and enhance public confidence.

Police reform and legislative change has opened up opportunities for police staff investigators who are now an integral part of police investigative teams and during an age of austerity, numbers are likely to increase.

PIP has contributed significantly to the professionalisation of police investigators at all levels of the police service, and together with the development of national competencies through the ICF, PIP has contributed to a growing professionalism of the role.

Recruitment, selection, training and assessment processes have been discussed and will provide any prospective candidate for an investigative post as a police officer or police staff, with some insight into the methods and processes adopted.

### CASE STUDY

*On this particular day, there are a number of detectives working a day shift. At the time the robbery is reported, the most senior, a detective inspector, is participating in a child abuse case conference at the local Social Services office. Two detective sergeants (DS) are on duty: one committed at the local Crown Court giving evidence in a criminal trial and another taking a refreshment break between working through a heavy administrative workload that includes checking crime reports, scrutinising* crime statistics and preparing an operational order for a drugs raid. There are also five DCs on duty: two are attending scenes of crime (two separate house burglaries), one is taking a statement regarding a credit card fraud and another is executing a search warrant to seize computer equipment connected with an allegation of distributing indecent images. The remaining DC is completing an arrest report in the CID office.

Officers attending the robbery at Roman's Newsagents request the attendance of a detective. In view of the seriousness of the crime being reported, police policy will usually dictate that it is the responsibility of the CID to take charge of this type of investigation.

The DS is tracked down in the police canteen and is requested to attend the scene of the robbery. He asks the DC in the CID to accompany him, and both attend the crime scene.

We have already witnessed considerable activity at the crime scene. The detective's first role is to establish exactly what has happened, what action has been taken and the results of any action taken. Security and preservation of the crime scene is paramount to maximise any forensic opportunities that may identify suspects and help build an accurate picture of events that took place during the commission of the crime.

Upon arrival, the two detectives are briefed by the officer in charge, a patrol sergeant. The importance of the golden hour has earlier been mentioned, and both detectives are pleased to find that appropriate action has been taken, that is:

- The crime scene has been cordoned off and a community support officer has been tasked with maintaining a log to record persons accessing the crime scene (this is crucial to maintain the integrity of the crime scene and to preserve forensic evidence).

- The crime scene investigator (CSI) has arrived quickly and is already starting to examine the crime scene.

- The victims have been taken to the nearby neighbourhood policing office and are making initial statements about the robbery.

- The witness who saw the suspects and provided a part vehicle registration mark is making a written statement.

- CCTV tapes from the newsagents have been secured and are readily available to be viewed. One of the foot-patrol officers has been despatched to the town's CCTV camera suite to check for any video evidence of the suspects.

The detectives are satisfied that the initial action taken by the policing team is in accordance with the best practice. The DS assumes overall responsibility for the investigation and then considers the subsequent steps to be taken. One of the immediate concerns is to trace the two suspects who are possibly armed and could still be a danger to the public. Action has already been taken to ensure an *appropriate police response should they be located so that the safety of both the public and the police is not compromised.*

*The DS makes contact with the local intelligence office to carry out an initial analysis of the crime and to identify any potential suspects. Arrangements are also made to carry out house-to-house enquiries in the vicinity of the robbery to find any further witnesses to the crime.*

*The CSI has made an initial assessment and informs the detectives that there is potential forensic evidence available such as fingerprints and footwear impressions that may be useful in identifying a suspect.*

*The DS obtains as much information about the crime as possible to brief senior officers who may have to make further decisions in relation to provision of resources, assist with developing an appropriate investigative strategy, preparing media statements and assessing the community impact of the crime.*

*The detectives are also concerned with securing all available evidence essential to secure a successful prosecution. This will include the ethical interviewing of witnesses to obtain detailed and accurate written statements that will stand scrutiny in court; the collection of exhibits that are properly recorded, packaged and secured; the recording of all investigative material; ensuring that any action taken is in accordance with legislation, codes of practice and local policing policy.*

## Self-assessment questions

1. Why was there a need to disband the Metropolitan Police detective division, and in which year was the CID first formed?

2. What allegations were made against detectives in a report in *The Times* in 1969, and which two Metropolitan Police Commissioners took positive action to tackle police corruption?

3. How did the Maxwell Confait appeal in 1975 contribute to the later RCCP 1978–81?

4. The PACE Act 1984 has eight codes of practice. What are they?

5. Name three miscarriages of justice and explain why the accused were able to win appeals against their convictions.

6. Name two pieces of legislation that resulted from recommendations made in 1993 by the Royal Commission following a review of the CJS.

7. What was the model of investigative interviewing introduced following the publication of the seven principles of investigating interviewing in 1992?

8. During the early years of police reform in the twenty-first century, what were the two new police bodies introduced to improve standards and encourage best practice?

9. What important doctrine was published by the NCPE in 2005?

10. What are the core responsibilities and behaviours provided by the policing professional framework for a DC?

*FURTHER READING*

Home Office Circular 22/92 (Principles of Investigative Interviewing)

*REFERENCES*

Association of Chief Police Officers (2005) *National Intelligence Model*. Wyboston: National Centre for Policing Excellence.

Baldwin, J (1992) *Video Taping Police Interviews with Suspects – an Evaluation*. Police Research Paper No. 1 London: Home Office.

Byford, L (1981) *The Yorkshire Ripper Case – Review of the Police Investigation of the Case*. London: Home Office.

Home Office (2001) *Policing a New Century: A Blueprint for Reform*. Norwich: Her Majesty's Stationery Office.

Home Office (2010) *Police and Criminal Evidence Act 1984 (PACE) and Accompanying Codes of Practice*. Available online at www.homeoffice.gov.uk/publications/police/operational-policing/pace-codes (accessed 20 December 2010).

Humphreys, S (2010) Personnel and Development Manager Shropshire 'F' Division. West Mercia Police: Interview 14 December 2010.

Macpherson, W (1999) *The Stephen Lawrence Inquiry*. London: The Stationery Office.

Nottinghamshire Police (2008) *Job Description – Support Investigator*. Available online at www.nottinghamshire.police.uk/uploads/vacancies/645/JD.pdf (accessed 14 December 2010).

NPIA National Police Improvement Agency (2010a) *PIP Implementation*. Available online at www.npia.police.uk/en/10094.htm (accessed 6 December 2010).

NPIA National Police Improvement Agency (2010b) *National Investigator's Examination*. Available online at www.npia.police.uk/en/13927.htm (accessed 16 December 2010).

Rawlings, P (2002) *Policing: A Short History*. Devon: Willan.

Reiner, R (2000) *The Politics of the Police*, 3rd edition. Oxford: Oxford University Press.

Research Development Statistics (2010) *Home Office – Various Statistical Reports Relating to 'Police Service Strength'*. Available online at http://rds.homeoffice.gov.uk/rds/index.html (accessed 14 December 2010).

Savage, S P (2007) *Police Reform – Forces for Change*. Oxford: Oxford University Press.

Shawyer, A, Milne, B and Bull, R (2009) Investigative Interviewing in the UK, chapter 2, in Williamson, T, Milne, B and Savage, S P (eds) *International Developments in Investigative Interviewing*. Devon: Willan.

Skills for Justice (2009) *Integrated Competency Framework 2009:Counter Terrorism*. Available online at http://icf.skillsforjustice.com/index.asp?SID=DBCBB108–7D0C-46AA-8A60–74855604DE68&PID=4&RPTGID=2 (accessed 17 December 2010).

Staffordshire Police (2009a) *Force Structure Protective Services*. Available online at www.staffordshire.police.uk/media/10810/foi/pdf/fsprotective (accessed 12 December 2010).

Staffordshire Police (2009b) *Force Structure Stoke on Trent*. Available online at www.staffordshire.police.uk/media/10810/foi/pdf/fssot (accessed 12 October 2010).

West Mercia Police (2010) *WM Investigative Officer (Operational)*. Major Investigation Unit – Role Profile.

*USEFUL WEBSITES*

www.acpo.police.uk (Association of Chief Police Officers).

www.npia.police.uk (National Police Improvement Agency).

www.skillsforjustice.com/default.asp?PageID=1 (Skills for Justice).

*LEGISLATION*

Criminal Appeals Act 1995.

Criminal Justice and Public Order Act 1994.

Criminal Procedure and Investigations Act 1996.

Police and Criminal Evidence Act 1984.

Police Reform Act 2002.

# 5 Using alternative tools for investigating crime

RACHAEL STRZELECKI

## CHAPTER OBJECTIVES

By the end of this chapter you will have:

- gained a knowledge and understanding of the history and development of intelligence and dedicated units within law enforcement agencies;
- gained a knowledge and understanding of the role of intelligence analysts and profilers;
- considered and analysed some of the issues and challenges that face an intelligence analyst or a profiler when helping police investigations.

## Introduction

This chapter explores the roles of those who work with information to create intelligence to assist in the investigation.

- Intelligence analysts.

- Profilers (behavioural and geographical).

The chapter considers the role of supporting units, more specifically, the intelligence units within local police forces and crime operational support units which work on a national scale. Both these departments help police investigations by working with and focusing on the intelligence that is being gathered by the other members of the investigative teams. The roles of the other team members have already been explained in earlier chapters. In this chapter, we are going to focus our attention on the following roles: first, the role of an intelligence analyst working for a local police force and second the role of a profiler, behavioural and geographical, who will aid with police investigations throughout the United Kingdom when needed. These roles will be illustrated when discussing the case study at the end of chapter.

# History of intelligence analysts and dedicated intelligence units within local police forces

Before examining the specific roles within intelligence units, it is important that they are considered in context by exploring the historical development of intelligence and dedicated units within law enforcement agencies. Intelligence is not a new phenomenon especially not in terms of policing and military. Sun Tzu's *The Art of War* was first published in 500 BC and contained the earliest recordings relating to espionage and military intelligence (Warner, 2002). In 1883, the Metropolitan Police introduced a special branch following a series of terrorist attacks by the Irish Fenian movement. During the 1960s, provincial police forces introduced their own special branch departments, and their main remit today is to acquire and develop intelligence to protect the public from national security threats, such as drug and human trafficking and terrorism or extremist activity. They also contribute to the challenge of promoting community safety and cohesion (Home Office, 2004). The Government Code and Cipher School was first established in 1919, becoming formally known as the Government Communications Headquarters (GCHQ) in 1946. Historically, this department has spent time breaking codes and developing cryptography (hiding information). It now deals with vast amounts of intelligence being received through information and communications technology systems. GCHQ's main aim is to provide intelligence, protect information and inform relevant UK policy to keep society safe and successful in the internet age. It works in close partnership with both MI5 and MI6. Although the primary customer for GCHQ intelligence products is the Ministry of Defence, it also works with the Foreign and Commonwealth Office and with local law enforcement agencies (Cabinet Office, 2009).

Historically, within local law enforcement agencies, the collection of intelligence was not as easy and as organised as it is today. The police relied on members of the public talking to them as they conducted their daily patrols. In 1928, however, the erection of dedicated 'police boxes' helped this intelligence-gathering process somewhat. These boxes were for the use of the police and the public to telephone through any reports of crime or incidents that may have occurred. These police boxes were an active part of the intelligence-gathering process until the 1960s (Metropolitan Police, 2010).

All law enforcement agencies worldwide now collect and collate all their essential data on computerised systems; however, that was not always the case. In the 1960s, law enforcement agencies started to use index cards to record vital pieces of information and intelligence. A call would come through to the call taker from either a member of the public or a police officer on duty and the information that was being given to the call taker would be written down by hand and placed on a conveyor belt that would take the information to the dispatcher's desk to be dealt with (Dempsey and Frost, 2009). It would be the job of a police collator to store and manage these index cards so that they would be close at hand when vital intelligence was needed. The collators were usually situated near the control room and had access to the police national computer records alongside the index cards. The information usually retained on these index cards were addresses, names, aliases, distinguishing mark and specific modus operandi that the individual used (Calder, 1980). Up until the early 1970s, there was no formal intelligence analysis unit; however, in 1971, Drexel Godfrey and Don Harris published *The Basic Elements of Intelligence* which outlined the key principles for an intelligence cycle. This cycle is still used by law enforcement agencies (Dunne, 2010).

Throughout the 1970s and 1980s, there were a number of reports published by Association of Chief Police Officers and the Home Office in relation to the use of intelligence within policing. In 1975, the Baumber Report was published that highlighted the requirement for co-ordinated information about serious, organised and cross-border crime. This was followed by the Pearce Report that led to the establishment of regional criminal intelligence offices. The Ratcliffe Report, published in 1986, led to the creation of a national drugs intelligence unit and the dedicated role of a field intelligence officer. Although the first analytical software was produced in the United States in 1985, it was not until the 1990s that operational analysis was being used within the United Kingdom (Griffiths, 2003). These reports led to the creation and implementation of the National Intelligence Model by which all police forces within the United Kingdom must adhere to, and it is the key model that underpins dedicated intelligence units within law enforcement agencies today.

Intelligence units within law enforcement agencies contain a variety of job roles including local intelligence officers, field intelligence officers, researchers, analysts, a detective sergeant and a detective inspector.

A local intelligence unit is run by a detective inspector and a detective sergeant and it is their role to co-ordinate the effective working of all the intelligence personnel under the guidance of the National Intelligence Model.

A local intelligence officer can either be a serving police officer or a member of the support staff, and they have the job of organising the information and intelligence that has been submitted for a particular area. They perform a variety of jobs including the creation of risk assessments on prisoners who are to be released back into the local area besides monitoring custody suits to identify potential local criminals who have recently been arrested who could be sources of intelligence.

A field intelligence officer, however, is a serving police officer, usually a detective with some years of experience. They have the responsibility of obtaining Covert Human Intelligence Sources (CHIS) and are usually out around the local area gathering intelligence and working closely with the proactive criminal investigation department (CID) teams.

A researcher is usually a member of the support staff of the organisation, and it is their role to research the intelligence and crime figures that will be used and interpreted by the analysts. In many intelligence units throughout the United Kingdom, the role of the researcher and the analyst can merge into one, with the analyst taking on much of the researching role. This can be owing to the paucity of staff in the department or the lack of understanding by the senior managers about the specific role descriptions of the staff.

# Who is an intelligence analyst?

An intelligence analyst is a qualified professional whose specific role is to analyse crime or intelligence data to influence specific decision makers usually within a law enforcement environment. An intelligence analyst provides analytical support to assist the local or force area in respect of crime patterns, crime trends, hot spots and offender details to identify an established or emerging crime series. They provide analytical support to assist with crime-prevention initiatives, targeting, disruption and detection of crime at a local and force level. Intelligence analysts work under the guidance of the National Intelligence Model producing analytical and intelligence products. It is the job of an analyst to influence the decision maker. Ratcliff (2008) uses a conceptual model to illustrate the role of an analyst when dealing with crime and law enforcement decision makers. The model shows how the analyst within the crime intelligence unit must interpret the criminal environment and must use a pull method to achieve the appropriate information and intelligence for collection. The model also demonstrates how the analyst must influence the thinking of the decision maker. Nicholl (2004) noted that there may be several decision makers, but it is vitally important for an analyst to identify the main decision maker so that terms of reference can be established for the requested task. Decision makers within local law enforcement are usually the divisional commanders of superintendent rank or senior managers of inspector rank and above. The final piece to this model is the impact that the decision maker has on the criminal environment. The ultimate goal is to reduce and prevent future crime; therefore, the decisions made by the decision maker are crucial if positive results are to be seen within the local area. It is, therefore, the main job of an analyst to be able to produce effective products and packages that can adequately equip the decision maker in making these crucial decisions.

# Job description

The following is a description of what a police service would be looking for when seeking to employ an intelligence analyst into the intelligence unit.

# Job purpose

To conduct tactical, strategic and operational analysis as part of the analytical team to support and inform the police service's approach to intelligence-led policing and delivery of the local policing plan.

# Principal duties and accountabilities

An intelligence analyst will be required to carry out a number of duties within their role, but their main area is to identify, plan and conduct collection and interpretation of information from a wide variety of sources relating to crime and incidents that are reported to the police, intelligence received from various sources such as Crimestoppers or Neighbourhood Watch, policing activities such as organised intelligence-gathering operations or from general policing duties and any other relevant law enforcement matters.

Alongside the collection and interpretation of data and intelligence, the analyst must also apply analytical techniques to develop hypotheses concerning the nature and scope of criminal activity, produce conclusions, identify intelligence gaps and make recommendations for action to assist the operational and strategic decision making process of police officers and police staff.

Another role that the intelligence analyst will undertake is the preparation of intelligence products. These include tactical, strategic and operational analytical and intelligence products and may also include work to support major incidents, investigations and crimes in action, presenting the results of the analysis in the most appropriate format and product. This can include written reports using corporate templates with charts, tables, graphs and so forth to display the crime figures or incidents being discussed. Moreover, an analyst has to, on occasion, verbally present their findings in the form of briefings which can include giving evidence for court. An intelligence analyst works with a variety of personnel both within the police organisation and alongside their multi-agency partners: personnel within intelligence, CID, neighbourhood policing and response staff, senior local- and force-level managers of all ranks, the Crown Prosecution Service, Crime and Disorder Reduction partnerships and the local councils.

In order for an analyst to carry out their role and duties, they need to maintain a flexible approach by demonstrating a willingness to adapt to changing circumstances such as secondment to another analytical team or specialist unit as the situation demands. This may include being placed within the major incident team (MIT) to aid and support their investigation. An analyst may also be required to spend time working within both level 1 (local level) and level 2 (force level) to gain experience in working at various levels within the organisation. An analyst is also expected to actively participate in briefings, meetings, seminars, workshops and conferences to gather and exchange information and intelligence. Within the job roles, the analyst must have a degree of personal responsibility and they must monitor their own work that they have been tasked with which include their daily duties within the team. It is also vital that the analyst identifies opportunities to improve both service provision and personal development and is expected to contribute to the continued development of the Force Analytical Function Team.

# What the role involves

Intelligence analysts were introduced to work with local officers who were polic-ing using intelligence. Since 2004, all police forces in England and Wales have been running their intelligence-led departments in accordance with the National Intelligence Model. This model was brought in to promote effective intelligence-led policing and to standardise the processes and products in England and Wales. There is now a uniform and systematic way in which all police forces handle and gather information and make decisions about the deployment of resources within each designated area (John and Maguire, 2004).

Under the guidance of the National Intelligence Model, tasking and co-ordination groups were set up. These groups are collectively made up of representatives from the intelligence units within the local police forces, senior officers with operational responsibilities (the decision makers) and multi-agency partners, for example, Crime and Disorder Reduction Partnerships. These members meet regularly, usually on a fortnightly basis at local level and every six weeks at force level, to undertake informed assessments and prioritisation of local problems including crime, crimi-nals, disorder and the opportunities for crime and plan, coordinate and manage police responses. In order for these decision makers to effectively perform their role, they use and request the further development of intelligence products, the contents and conclusions of which should underpin both prioritisation and opera-tional decisions.

An analyst's key role within the tasking and co-ordination group process is the production of intelligence products. There are four key products produced by the analytical team:

1. Tactical assessment – This supports specific operations by examining short-term problems within the local community, monitors existing and emerging pat-terns and trends, helps target offenders and offending behaviour, and makes reasoned judgements recommendations for crime reduction and resource deployment.

2. Strategic assessment – This is used to inform policy by analysing long-term problems and identifying areas of strength, weakness, opportunity, threat and risk. It also helps identify potential scope for criminal activity.

3. Target profile – This is a person-specific package that analyses the information about a particular person who is of interest to the police. Data within this pack-age includes personal details, criminal history, associations with other known criminals, financial information and any risk assessments that have previously been conducted.

4. Problem profile – This package is specific to a particular problem that has been identified, for example, increased crime within a particular area. This package is quite detailed and will include any patterns that have been identified with the area, the specific crimes and modi operandi that have been used, the main days and times that the offences or incidents were committed, the locations

and potential victims in case there is an emerging pattern, offender analysis of potential suspect that could be considered for the offences and recommendations to the decision makers that may help reduce the crime or prevent it from occurring in the future.

(Research and Intelligence Support Centre, 2006)

Besides producing intelligence products for the tasking and co-ordination group, an analyst must carry out daily tasks which involve the production of analytical products. There are nine key analytical products that have been identified under the National Intelligence Model (Table 5.1).

# Qualifications

This is down to the discretion of the individual police force, but the minimum that would be required is five GCSE grades A–C. However, most applicants have a good undergraduate degree in social science or a related subject such as criminology, crime and investigation, psychology or law.

# Recruitment into the role

There is a four-step process for recruitment into the role of an intelligence analyst from outside the police service. First, the applicant must have the appropriate qualifications that have been requested by the police force. If you are successful through the application process, then you will be invited to an assessment day where you will complete tests to show that you have the skills and abilities needed to become an analyst. These tests also show that you are competent in both mathematics and English. Third, if you successfully complete this assessment day, then you will be invited back for an interview which includes some form of presentation. When you arrive at the interview venue, you are given a case-study scenario and allowed time to compile a presentation to present your findings to the interview panel. The first portion of the interview is the presentation of your case-study findings, and the latter part of the interview is a series of questions put to you by the interview panel. Finally, if you have been successful through the interview process, then you will be subject to a vetting process. This looks into your background and that of your family to identify if you or any members of your family have any criminal convictions or been involved in any criminal activities that could compromise your position working within a secure intelligence unit of a police force. If you have met all the requirements of the vetting, then you will be formally offered the role of an intelligence analyst.

The role of an analyst can also be applied for from within the police service. This will usually happen with data or intelligence researchers who are looking to move up into the role of an analyst. In this instance, the applicant will submit the application form, attend an assessment day and be interviewed by the panel. There is no need to go through the vetting process as the applicant already works for the organisation.

*Table 5.1 The nine key analytical products*

| Analytic product | Main function |
| --- | --- |
| Crime pattern analysis | A crime pattern analysis looks for any links between crimes, incidents, victims, offenders and the like for any similarities or indeed differences that could potentially help solve the crime or problem highlighted. It is a generic term for a collection of related crime or incident series identification, crime-trend analysis, hot spot analysis and general profile analysis |
| Criminal business profile | This contains a detailed analysis of how a criminal operation is run, much like that of a legal business. The profile identifies all the aspects of the criminal business including the modus operandi, victims, technical processes involved, the commodity, its transportation and routes, methods of disposing and laundering the profits and proceeds and it will identify any potential weaknesses that will help bring down the business |
| Demographic and social trend analysis | This product focuses on the demographic changes and the impact that it has on criminality. This product also analyses social factors such as housing and unemployment and how this links to the changes in crime. It also identifies population shifts and how they can be used to ensure effective community partnerships |
| Market profile analysis | This product is an assessment of the criminal market surrounding a particular commodity such as a stolen vehicle. It analyses the potential market, availability, price, individuals involved, any networks or associations, criminal assets or trends that can be linked with the crime |
| Network analysis | This identifies links between individuals who are persons of interest to the police. It also identifies the significance of the links between each of the associates and the particular roles that each of the individuals have within the network. Through analysis, the strengths and weaknesses of the criminal organisation can also be identified and it can also identify if there are any links with other known criminal businesses or organisations |
| Operational intelligence assessment | This product evaluates incoming intelligence for a particular operation that has had previously set objectives. This helps to identify any gaps that may be occurring within the operation or any further intelligence priorities that need to be identified for the operation |
| Results analysis | A results analysis evaluates the effectiveness of particular strategies or initiatives that have been carried out. This product can assist in the identification of best practice or identify areas for improvement |
| Risk analysis | This product is rarely done solely by an analyst but will be completed with a member of the intelligence staff such as an intelligence or field officer. The product assesses the risk that a particular individual or a particular victim, criminal organisation, law enforcement or the local environment poses |

*Table 5.1 (Continued)*

| Analytic product | Main function |
|---|---|
| Target profile analysis | This product includes a range of analytical techniques focused on a particular offender. It will identify the individual and their preferred criminal activity, associations, lifestyle, risk assessments and potential for offending. This product can also identify gaps that need to be filled in relation to intelligence needed on the target |

# Skills and qualities

There are certain skills and qualities that an analyst is required to have in order to be able to perform their role effectively. An analyst is required to have a good standard of education including excellent numeracy and literacy skills. These key skills must demonstrate exemplary interpersonal communication skills, including presentation skills, both verbal and written. An analyst must also have the ability to solve problems and work effectively when put under pressure. These are crucial skills as some roles that an analyst must undertake, such as working with the MIT, will be demanding and require working to tight deadlines and producing accurate products suitable as evidence in court. As a large proportion of an analyst's work is conducted on computerised systems, an analyst is required to be IT literate and should have a good working knowledge of using spreadsheets and Word processing packages. Another vital skill that is required is the ability to use statistical methods and reasoning, and to have an understanding of charts and tables and the ability to interpret and develop inferences from data.

An analyst, although part of a dedicated team, must also be able to work as effectively alone. On occasion an analyst will be required to work on solo projects producing specific packages for local or force manager. It is, therefore, essential that an analyst be able to work with minimum supervision but remain as part of a focused team. The final quality that an analyst must have to be able to perform in the role is the ability to be self-motivated and be able to use initiative when conducting analytical work and producing packages and products for local or force managers.

# Training

Once you are in the role of an analyst, you will be trained in the basic analytical software used by the police force. In addition to the software training, the analyst has to complete the basic analyst training, which includes legislation and practices relevant to the role, and analytical packages and profiles that are used by the analyst. Also included in this initial training is the background and history for intelligence, analytical work and how they help and work with law enforcement agencies.

# Potential for role and career progression

The analytical unit consists of data researchers, analysts, a senior analyst and a principal analyst. They are all civilian support staff who are there to aid the local law enforcement teams. The principal analyst has overall responsibility for the analysts and researchers within their particular division or force area. The size of the police force will determine the size of the analytical support staff unit, thus determining how many managers or principal analysts are needed. The principal analyst works together with crime managers, usually at the rank of superintendent, and works towards attaining the strategic goals of the police force that are documented within the local policing plan for that particular force area. The principal analyst will also oversee any operations that may be going on that involve any intelligence analyst or senior analyst working within a major incident such as a murder or rape or operations that are being conducted by Special Branch. The senior analyst answers to the principal analyst and works with the local crime managers and is responsible for the intelligence analysts and the researchers within the intelligence units.

Intelligence analysts have a lot of potential within the role. After the basic training and some experience is gained, work permitting, the analyst can focus or specialise on specific crime types such as volume crime, major incidents or ongoing operations within Special Branch. After an analyst is trained within law enforcement, the potential for the role is considerable nationally. However, the jobs that are available are few, such as working in the Serious Crime Analysis Section that analyses rape, serious sexual assault and sexually motivated murders, or within the crime operations support units as geographical or behavioural profilers.

# Using profiling to solve crimes

During the 1980s, scientists started helping police investigation in an attempt to catch the criminals before they committed further offences. It has previously been suggested by Shaw and McKay (1942) that most criminals will only commit crime within a short distance of where they live. However, more recently, this idea has been questioned due to certain high-profile cases such as the Yorkshire Ripper. Scientists found that they could estimate the location of the offenders based upon analysis of particular geographical locations of the crimes that they had committed. This possible area where the offender would be located is what Canter (2004) noted as geographical profiling.

Since the early 1970s, in the United States, insights into psychological science have been applied to criminal behaviour to what has become known as 'behavioural profiling'. This is a science that allows you to understand a criminal, who they are, what they think when they are committing a crime and why indeed they have committed the crime in the first instance. All this information can be used to detect crime (Federal Bureau of Investigation, 2010).

Geographical and behavioural profiling are used in conjunction with each other to help solve crimes within the United Kingdom. The role of the geographical profiler is more commonly used within police investigations in the United Kingdom. For recruitment into either role within the United Kingdom, the applicant must have been an crime or either intelligence analyst who has gained experience working on major incidents such as murders or rapes or must have gained extensive knowledge of working alongside police conducting investigative work. The applicant may also be a serving police officer with at least three years' experience working in an investigative role and must have the appropriate qualifications that are required, such as a degree in either social sciences or a related subject such as criminology or psychology. Both roles are described in the ensuing sections.

# Who is a geographical profiler?

A geographical profiler is a technically trained and qualified individual. Currently within the United Kingdom, there are four geographical profilers who work within the North, South, East and West regions. In order to effectively do their job, they need to visit the various crime scenes. A geographical profiler can locate the residences of offenders or specific locations where the offender may be based up, conduct analysis on the crimes, and deduce the days and times that they were committed. A geographical profiler is used in major investigations such as when investigating a murder. When using geographical analysis, the profiler analyses the locations of a series of linked crimes in detail and looks for the characteristics of the area, for example, the neighbourhoods in which they have occurred.

Not every case that a geographical profiler gets called out to is suitable for a search analysis, so the profiler will generally conduct a preliminary review to establish whether they can create a profile and help the investigation. From earlier work, however, the following crime types have been successful and suitable to geographical profiling.

- Murder.

- Rape and sexual assault.

- Abduction.

- Arson.

- Bombings and explosive devices.

- Robbery.

- Burglary.

- Multiple location crime, for example, the use of credit cards.

The role of a geographical profiler is continually being developed and improved, with the latest technique of Geographical Search Analysis being modified. This technique will assist the geographical profiler in finding the missing bodies of individuals who are suspected of being murdered but where a body has never been found. This technique involves the analysis of the days, times and locations of the crimes combined with the intelligence that has been gained about the suspected offenders, their movements, background, lifestyles and so forth. All these factors combined give the investigators a list of locations or probable sites where the body could be found. A similar technique that is also used when searching for a missing suspect is Target Location Analysis. This is conducted in a similar way to the technique just described.

A geographical profiler will also be able to give Mapping Assistance. This is useful when plotting a number of offences or crimes that have been linked in a series. It is also beneficial when investigating historical cases that need to be plotted and viewed for evidentiary purposes in briefings or in court.

Although a geographical profiler can work alone on a case to provide the location of the offender or the missing body, the compiled profile is more accurate and effective when combined with the analysis of the behavioural profiler.

## Who is a behavioural profiler?

Behavioural profilers or behavioural investigative advisors, as they are known within the National Police Improvements Agency where they are employed, provide support and advice to the investigation, linking the theory behind behavioural science to the actual investigation of serious crimes. The profiler will advise an investigation on several elements including the following.

- Crime scene assessment.

- Motivational factors.

- Cold case reviews.

- Series identification/case linkage.

- Risk assessments.

- DNA screening suspect prioritisation.

- Interview strategy.

- Offender background characteristics.

- Investigative suggestions/strategies.

(National Police Improvement Agency, 2010)

The support of the behavioural profiler is provided only at the request of the senior investigating officer (SIO). After the request has been made, the profiler will attend the scene(s) of crime with a crime investigation support officer and will receive a briefing from the SIO. The profiler will then request and collate all the relevant case materials that are needed to compile a profile of the suspect. These materials include information and statements from the victim(s), witnesses(s), photographs that have been taken of the crime scene, pathology reports and photographs that have been taken post-mortem and any relevant intelligence that the investigative team has gathered. The behavioural profiler then compiles a report on the crime. They use the material they have gathered and collated from the investigative team, academic research, analysis of relevant databases that they have access to, relevant sources of information and other leading experts in the field so that an accurate profile of the offender can be gained. The finished report is submitted to the SIO, usually in conjunction with the report from the geographical profiler.

**C H A P T E R   S U M M A R Y**

This chapter has provided a historical overview of intelligence, intelligence analysts and the dedicated intelligence units within law enforcement agencies. The relevant government papers published on intelligence gathering, demonstrating the need to improve intelligence working and sharing within the law enforcement agencies, were also documented.

The role of an intelligence analyst was greatly focused upon, and it is an essential role within local law enforcement agencies and a ground role for other professions such as geographical profiling. Analysts play a crucial role within the tasking and co-ordination group processes producing key intelligence products. In addition to that role, analysts also create a number of analytical products that aid other police investigations at a local or force level.

The role of profiling is a relatively new phenomenon within the United Kingdom, but in recent years, the role has proved to be a vital tool for police investigations. The combination of geographical and behavioural profiling looks at the possible locations and psychological background of the offender in order to find the most suitable place that the offender or the victim of the crime could be located. Improvements within these job roles are continually occurring and are being used, when appropriate, more readily in everyday police investigations.

---

**CASE STUDY**

*Now that you fully understand the alternative methods and tools for investigating crime, you can now see how it works in practice. Our case study continues …*

*The intelligence unit was promptly informed by a detective from the CID that there was a potential armed robbery at Roman's Newsagents on High Street in the centre of town. The inspector, sergeant and senior analyst call a meeting in the intelligence office to brief the team. The facts that are known so far are:*

* *There are two male suspects. The first male is described as five feet ten inches tall, wearing a red and white striped football top, and black tracksuit bottoms*

*and black tracksuit jacket. Male is IC1 with black spiked hair. The second suspect is approximately five feet tall, IC3, with a shaven head, wearing a blue t-shirt, white tracksuit top and blue jeans.*

* *The suspects are believed to have fled in a red Ford Focus, registration number TU10 XXX, which is believed to have been stolen prior to the offence being committed.*

* *The CSI has been to the scene and has recovered footwear impressions, fibres and fingerprints which have all been sent for analysis.*

*The local intelligence officers, the field officers and the analysts set to work to identify the suspects.*

*The field officers leave the office to go and speak to known CHIS within the M1 area to try and gain some vital and actionable intelligence, while the local intelligence officers get to work searching for historical intelligence that could potentially suggest that this armed robbery was going to take place.*

*The analysts start by searching through their databases for males matching that description that have been sighted and stop-checked by police officers in the area in the hours leading up to the offence. Further searches are also conducted on the recorded crimes databases to establish whether there have been similar robberies committed within the M1 area, in the neighbouring divisions or force wide. Searches are also conducted on the motor vehicles that have been stolen within the M1 area.*

*After a short time, the results of the search start to come back. There are no matches to the descriptions of the males found on the stop-check database. However, there are five results of similar offences found within the force area as shown in Table 5.2 below.*

*Table 5.2  Results for similar offences*

| Offence | Location | Time | Property stolen | Description of offenders |
|---|---|---|---|---|
| Robbery | M3, Barry's Newsagents and Deli – Broad Street, Newham | 12:00 | £326 cash from the till | Two males, one with black hair wearing a tracksuit approximately five feet nine and one with a shaved head about five feet with a local accent |
| Attempted robbery | S1, Post office – High Street, Shilton | 13:35 | No property | Two males in tracksuits. One male was white, and the second male had a shaved head |
| Robbery | L1, Matilda's Muffin Shop – High Street, Longhampton | 14:15 | £159 cash from the till, 26 boxes of cigarettes and several bottles of alcohol | Two males approximately late teens. One male was approximately five feet ten with dark hair and the other male was approximately five feet with a shaved head and spoke with a local accent |

| Robbery | S2, Brown's Newsagent – New Street, South Shilton | 13:45 | £281 cash from the till and 15 boxes of cigarettes | Two males both with local accents, one with dark hair and one with a shaved head. Both approximately 20 year old wearing tracksuits and football tops |
| Robbery | H1, Molly's Local Shop – High Street, Hardwick | 13:00 | £327 cash from the till, two large bottles of spirits and four packets of tobacco | Two males, one white and one Asian wearing tracksuits and spoke with a local accent |

*A crime pattern analysis (CPA) product is then rapidly produced to give an in-depth analysis of these offences. As shown in the table above, there are five similar descriptions to the males that were sighted committing the robbery at the newsagents. There are also similarities between the locations of the offences, the times that they were committed and the type of property that was stolen.*

*As these offences have been committed throughout the force area, the analyst contacts the local intelligence offices within these other divisions to see if they have any intelligence or potential suspects that could aid this investigation. While waiting for these results, the local intelligence officer retrieves a historical intelligence log from the neighbourhood watch archives which reads …*

*This is probably nothing but I heard my next door neighbour's son and a few f[r]iends of his talking and laughing in their backyard while I was hanging out my washing and I thought I heard Petey saying that they were going to rob a shop in town. I may have been mistaken as I am 84 and my hearing is going but I think that is what they said. Petey is such a sweet boy and I don't think that he would be involved with such things but his friends look like bad news.*

*An address was found for this neighbourhood watch member through the neighbourhood watch co-ordinator, and it was established that Petey resided at 48, Amble Street, but had no prior convictions. Further searches in the stop-check database, however, found that Petey or Peter Sramford had been stop-checked on several occasions, usually during the weekend evenings within the M1 area, in the company of three friends, George Ellis, Asif Mohammad and Jan Namisowictz.*

*A target profile was then created for these three individuals which identified that Namisowictz had no police record; however, Ellis had several convictions for shoplifting, burglary and robbery, and Mohammad had previous record for vehicle crime, predominately theft of motor vehicles. From these target profiles, the analyst then makes a good reasoned judgement that Ellis and Mohammad are the potential suspects.*

*Mohammad is a prolific vehicle criminal, but from previous intelligence received, he always dumps the stolen vehicles in the same area. A map is produced using mapping software that pinpoints the locations of Mohammad's car thefts and the dumpsites of these stolen vehicles. The map shows that there is only one road that leads to his favoured dumpsite. With this information, the analysts takes the maps, the CPA and the target profiles to the senior analyst, and the detective inspector and recommends that automatic number plate recognition is notified to identify the vehicle when it is heading down Southlands Road towards the dumpsite which in turn could lead to the vehicle being stopped.*

# Self-assessment questions

1. Which year saw the first publication of tactical intelligence?

2. In which year did intelligence gathering and reporting become easier in the United Kingdom with the erection of police boxes?

3. Prior to the implementation of computerised systems, how was intelligence recorded and stored?

4. Who outlined the main principles of the intelligence cycles that are still used today?

5. Which model is best used to describe the role of an analyst?

6. Since 2004, all forces in England and Wales have been running their intelligence-led departments in accordance with which model?

7. How many analytical products are available for police investigations?

8. How many geographical profilers are, currently, working in the United Kingdom?

9. Can geographical profiling be used on any crime?

10. By what other name is a behavioural profiler known within the United Kingdom?

REFERENCES

Cabinet Office (2009) *Intelligence Agencies*. Available online at www.cabinetoffice.gov.uk/intelligence-security-resilience/national-security.aspx (accessed 12 August 2010).

Calder, J (1980) *Policing the Police*, Volume 2. Oxford: Hart Publishing.

Canter, D (2004) Geographic Profiling of Criminals. *Medico-legal Journal*, 72(2): 53–66.

Dempsey, J and Frost, L (2009) *An Introduction to Policing*, 5th edition. New York: Deimar.

Dunne, R (2010) *The Intelligence Cycle*. Available online at http://ukcrimeanalysis.blogspot.com/2010/11/intelligence-cycle.html (accessed 12 February 2011).

Federal Bureau of Investigation (2010) *Behavioural Science*. Available online at www.fbi.gov/about-us/training/bsu (accessed 17 February 2011).

Griffiths, I (2003) *Intelligence: Best Value Review*. Wales: Dyfed-Powys Police.

Home Office (2004) *Guidelines on Special Branch Work in the United Kingdom*. London: HMSO.

John, T and Maguire, M (2004) *The National Intelligence Model: Key Lessons from Early Research*. London: Home Office.

Metropolitan Police (2010) *The History of the Metropolitan Police*. Available online at www.met.police.uk/history/index.htm (accessed 14 February 2011).

National Police Improvement Agency (2010) *Crime Operational Support*. Available online at www.npia.police.uk/en/5220.htm (accessed 17 February 2011).

Nicholl, J (2004) Task Definition, in Ratcliffe, J *Strategic Thinking in Criminal Intelligence*. Sydney: Federation Press.

Ratcliffe, J (2008) *Intelligence-Led Policing*. Devon: Willan Publishing.

Research and Intelligence Support Centre (2006) *The UK National Intelligence Model 2006 and Beyond*. Middlesex, UK: Research and Intelligence Support Centre.

Shaw, C and McKay, H (1942) *Juvenile Delinquency and Urban Areas*. Chicago: University of Chicago Press.

Warner, M (2002) Wanted: A Definition of Intelligence. *Studies in Intelligence*. 46(3): 15–23.

# 6  The RPU officer, ANPR operator, road death/collision investigator and AFO

RUTH MCGRATH

### CHAPTER OBJECTIVES

By the end of this chapter you will be able to:

- differentiate between the roles of the road policing unit officer, the automated number plate recognition operator, the road death/collision investigator and the authorised firearms officer;
- list some of the functions performed by the road policing unit, and associated roles;
- interpret statistical information relating to collisions and potential causes;
- state how the use of the automated number plate recognition can assist the police service.

## Introduction

This chapter explores the functions of those who police and deal with incidents on the roads.

- Road policing unit (RPU) officer.

- Automated number plate recognition (ANPR) operator.

- Road death/collision investigator.

- Authorised firearms officer (AFO).

The media often portrays police officers as driving everywhere at high speed, chasing and catching criminals. In fact, there is much more to the policing role as you will already be beginning to realise. This chapter explores the development of the specialist roles of the RPU officer (police officer), collision investigator (police officer or civilian), the ANPR operator (police officer or civilian) and the armed response officer (police officer). It will compare their broad range of roles and functions within the police service, and how their work supports each other and in particular their potential role within the investigation of the robbery at Roman's Newsagents in High Street as our case study continues.

It is as motorists that many members of the public have their first direct experience of the police. A 1976 study established that 39 per cent of all drivers surveyed had been spoken to by a police officer about a possible offence, 25 per cent of those having been spoken to more than once in the preceding 30 months (Griffiths et al., 1980). A later study showed that the enforcement of traffic legislation by the police can lead to significant increases in road safety (Elliott and Broughton, 2005), although James and Nahl (2000) suggest that marked patrol cars will only have a deterrent effect when they are actually present. It is suggested that the ever-increasing growth of legislation relevant to use of the road is reliant upon enforcement by the police (Dix and Layzell, 1983).

These statements serve to offer some indication of the importance of the role of the RPU and allied specialist roles, and will be explored in more detail as we progress through this chapter. It is useful to begin by examining the development of the use of motor vehicles within the context of policing.

# A brief history of police motor vehicles

The Metropolitan Police introduced the first police vehicle in 1858 – a horse-drawn secure carriage which was used as a prison van for escorting detained persons. It became known as a *Black Maria*, a nickname which is believed to originate from Boston, Massachusetts in the 1830s, after a black lodging-house keeper named Maria Lee who used to assist constables in escorting drunks to cells (Metropolitan Police Service, n.d.).

Early documentation of road congestion in London leading to enforcement by the police is known to have been taking place as early as the 1850s. A police officer's notebook from this period contains entries making references to unlicensed bus conductors being served summons, in addition to being served summons for offences relating to having excess passengers or not picking up passengers. Cab drivers are also recorded as *loitering* and driving their carriages while drunk (Emsley, 2009).

Arden et al. (2008) suggest that one of the first motor vehicles owned by the Metropolitan Police was a Crossley Buggy Car, around 1901. However, this would not have been used for patrolling; it is more likely to have been used to transport the commissioner around the area.

In the 1920s, prosecution of drivers of speeding motor vehicles increased to such an extent that the courts began to have difficulty dealing with the number of cases (Emsley, 1993). Public opposition to traffic police enforcing speeding legislation increased, leading to an intervention from the then home secretary, asking chief constables not to treat motorists as criminals. By 1930, the Road Traffic Act abolished the speed limit for most vehicles, partially as a result of reduced crashes. This was a short-term measure, and in 1934 the Road Transport Act introduced a speed restriction of 30 mph in urban areas (Corbett, 2003).

It was possibly not until as late as the 1930s that police motor vehicles began to be used on a regular basis around the country for the purpose of patrol or responding to incidents. Since then a range of vehicles have been used, most police forces selecting models which appeared most appropriate to their needs.

The Metropolitan Police introduced the specific role of the traffic police around 1929. At this time, police officers either rode motorcycles or drove cars in the pursuit of their employment. Vehicles selected for traffic use tended to be larger in size with a capability of reaching a higher speed, and generally of a higher specification than a general patrol vehicle. This reflected the differing nature of their use.

Police driving instruction was not introduced until the 1930s. Lord Trenchard took up appointment as commissioner of the Metropolitan Police in 1931, a role he carried out until 1935. During this period, he established a police training college at Hendon and, with guidance from Sir Malcolm Campbell, then holder of the land speed record, established police driving instruction (Stead, 1985). This training assisted officers to deal with the increasing number of incidents involving vehicles, including collisions, injuries and deaths, while enabling greater mobility to deal with crime. Driver training has developed since then and is now guided by the Police Driving Manual (ACPO/ACPOS, 2009).

It was not until after the Second World War that traffic divisions, today known as RPUs, were generally introduced in police forces around the country.

Despite the presence of traffic divisions, motor vehicles were not used as a routine tool to police local areas until the 1960s when the chief constable of Lancashire, Eric St Johnson (one of Trenchard's protégés in the 1930s), realised that it was not possible to police areas effectively with the number of officers generally available (six officers to police 11 beat areas). He experimented in Kirby, placing foot patrols only in the town centre and dividing the remaining area into five mobile beat areas, supported by pocket radios. So successful was the experiment that by the end of the 1960s, it was being used across most of the country (Emsley, 2009).

Having considered some of the historical aspects of police vehicles, let us now focus more on the role of the RPU.

# The road policing unit

*Policing professional framework (Skills for Justice, 2011)*

**Road policing constable (a police officer)**
To carry out this role, you must be a competent constable

**A Road policing constable must be able to:**
• provide an initial response to road-related incidents;
• prepare and drive patrol and response vehicles;
• stop vehicles while driving;
• deal safely and effectively with vehicles which fail to stop.

**Personal qualities**
• Decision making.
• Leadership.
• Professionalism.
• Public service.
• Working with others.

As you will have already seen, the generic function of police officers is to:

• protect life and property;

• preserve order;

• prevent the commission of offences;

• bring offenders to justice;

• perform any duty or responsibility arising from common or statute law.

(ACPO, 2007a)

Within this section, you will begin to consider the more focused role of the road policing officer.

The report 'Roads Policing and Technology: Getting the Right Balance' defines the police traffic (road policing) function, dividing it into three key areas.

1. Operational – police officers patrolling either on motorcycles or in patrol vehicles policing traffic and motorway patrol duties;

2. Operational support – staff who support the operational role, with responsibilities such as accident investigation, speed detection, vehicle examination, traffic administration and hazardous chemicals;

3. Organisational support – administrative staff supporting the traffic function.

(House of Commons Transport Committee, 2006)

Some of these functions are carried out by regular patrol officers and some by members of the staff who are not sworn police officers. However, some functions require more specialised knowledge and skills, and we will be examining some of these roles further in this chapter.

Despite variations between forces, most (although not all) police forces have RPUs. Their structure may include dedicated motorcyclists, patrol officers who drive the cars, armed response officers and collision investigation officers. In many forces, the RPU also has AFOs within its unit.

In recent years, the government has transferred some of the responsibilities of road policing to non-sworn officers working within other agencies. One example is that of policing motorway traffic. While police officers are still allocated to motorway patrols, the Highways Agency Traffic Officers now have responsibility for generally managing congestion, removing obstructions and assisting vulnerable road users. More recently, the Highways Agency has also introduced the Incident Support Unit function which offers an enhanced service on a local level often managed by private companies.

Another form of transferring of responsibilities is that of *decriminalising* some offences on the roads. This means such offences are no longer regarded by society as *crimes*. An example would be that of parking offences. Once the responsibility of the police, local authorities will now deal with parking offences. Still regarded as a breach of legislation, such offences will now be dealt with by means of a fine rather than being addressed within the criminal justice system.

The transferring of responsibilities has had the effect of reducing some of the pressure upon RPU officers, freeing them to deal with more serious matters, or offering specific support such as road closures at incidents.

The RPU will, however, always retain primary responsibility for the following areas.

- Injury or death.
- Criminality.
- Threats to public order and safety.
- Allegations of criminality or threats to public order and safety.
- Significant co-ordination of emergency responders.

(ACPO, 2007a)

To become a police officer within the RPU, there is an expectation that you will have already undertaken your initial police learning and development programme and completed your two-year probationary period. You will be expected to have acquired a general understanding of legislation and procedures prior to making your application for transfer and also hold a current driving licence.

Following your posting, you will, over a period of time, be given additional training to develop a detailed knowledge of traffic-related legislation, vehicle examination, basic collision investigation and scene management and relevant local procedures. You will be given specific training to increase your driving skills to Advanced Driver status. You will also receive role-specific training, for example, to be able to use specific equipment such as speed-detection devices and the Stinger device. If specialising further, for example, as an armed response officer, an ANPR operator, collision investigation officer or motorcyclist, then you will undergo further specific training to develop expertise in these areas. It is not unusual for officers to develop specialist skills in more than one area.

RPU officers work shift patterns which vary from force to force, and which may differ from those of local colleagues, but generally provide cover 24 hours a day, seven days a week. They tend to patrol a greater area than that of their response policing colleagues, crossing district boundaries and in some cases across police force boundaries, particularly where forces share the road policing function.

RPUs contribute to a number of key functions in partnership with a range of other agencies such as the Highways Agency, local councils, and voluntary and community bodies. These include:

- denying criminals use of the roads by enforcing the law;

- reducing road casualties;

- tackling the threat of terrorism;

- reducing anti-social use of the roads;

- enhancing public confidence and reassurance by patrolling the roads.

(Home Office, 2010)

As might be expected, maintaining the safety of road users (both in vehicles and as pedestrians) is an important function for the RPU, one which encompasses reducing the risk of road users becoming casualties. Research is ongoing to establish the accuracy of suggested links between excess speed and collisions (Richards et al., 2010). There are indications that the higher the speed of a vehicle, the greater the likelihood of injury (Richards, 2010). This information is, however, disputed by use of alternative figures and press reports at regular intervals (Mason, 2003).

Despite this, for some years now, there has been an ongoing aim in most areas of the country to reduce incidents of speeding. This has been dealt with by different approaches. Nationally, the media has been engaged in the education of the public, sending out messages informing them of the dangers of speeding. At local levels, high-visibility policing is used, for example, placing a marked police vehicle on a motorway overpass, and using speed-detection devices in a variety of forms, namely, using radar, laser or GPS signals to measure the speed of a moving vehicle. They may be hand-held devices which look similar to an oversized handgun and which are used when the operator is static, or devices fitted into RPU vehicles which enable the user to be moving as well. Mobile speed-detection cameras are those fitted into adapted vehicles and which may also be static.

Fixed speed-detection cameras are also used in many forces around the country to assist in the process of reducing speed and thereby reducing casualties. The operation of these cameras, and subsequent processing of information gathered by them, is often overseen by non-sworn staff (Sheldon and Wright, 2010).

Detection of speeding offences may lead to the issuing of a fixed penalty ticket that requires the driver to surrender their driving licence to enable penalty points to be added in addition to the payment of a fine. The National Speed Awareness Scheme is offered to offending drivers only marginally over the speed limit, giving them the opportunity to attend an awareness-raising training session as an alternative to the fine and penalty points (Stephenson et al., 2010). Alternatively, a driver might receive summons to attend the Magistrates Court.

At times there might be a requirement to safely escort *abnormal loads* along main routes. These are vehicles which may be longer, wider or higher than standard. In some cases, their load may be such that it overhangs the edges of the trailer carrying it, which may present some risk to other motorists. However, this function is no longer a routine police responsibility, largely being conducted by other agencies engaged by hauliers.

RPU officers are required to deal with vehicle collisions, although the more serious situations will be dealt with specifically by the collision investigation officers. This role will be explored in more detail later in this chapter.

As has already been referred to, casualty reduction is a major goal of the RPU. Key methods of approaching this include enforcement, punishment, tactical and high-visibility patrols, use of closed circuit television (CCTV) to detect offenders, reports from members of the public and education and publicity campaigns (Rogers and Lewis, 2007).

The latter might include participation in specific operations, in conjunction with other agencies. These might include local authority representatives, the Royal Society for the Prevention of Accidents or the road safety charity, Brake. The police continue to be involved in a number of awareness initiatives, such as the National Driver Offender Re-Training Scheme, a court diversion scheme and allowing a chief constable to introduce educational courses as an alternative to prosecution for certain offences. While schemes vary around the country, some examples of such schemes are as follows.

- The Driver Improvement Scheme (DIS).

- The Rider Intervention Development Experience (RiDE).

- The Speed Awareness Course (SAC).

(Cleveland Police, 2010)

At different times of the year, the RPU might be engaged in specific casualty reduction initiatives. Some campaigns are agreed to at a local level, whereas others are part of national initiatives. Examples of national initiatives include campaigns to reduce drink-driving usually taking place during the Christmas period, to reduce incidents of speeding and to increase the regular use of seat belts. Such initiatives are agreed to within the Traffic Information System Police (TISPOL), an organisation formed to exchange traffic information between Europe's capital cities and supported by the European Commission. Locally, campaigns might entail working in partnership with agencies such as the Vehicle Inspectorate to conduct checks to ensure the roadworthiness of vehicles. Focused campaigns inform and educate members of the public, raising awareness of issues which may otherwise be forgotten or overlooked.

Drink-driving and drug-driving continue to be issues affecting the safety of road users. Testing equipment has existed for many years. Today, sophisticated hand-held devices can be used to conduct roadside breath tests and will give an instant reading indicating levels of alcohol in the breath tested. Ongoing trials continue to be conducted to establish the most effective form of detecting drugs and their levels in the body. Use of reliable equipment would increase the number of detected incidences of drugs and could assist in the reduction of drug-driving.

---

R E F L E C T I V E   T A S K

*Consider the following information which makes for interesting reading.*

- *In 1926, there were 1,715,000 motor vehicles registered and 4,886 road fatalities.*
  *(Hicks and Allen, 1999)*

- *In 2009, the number of licensed vehicles in Great Britain had increased to over 34 million, with an average increase of more than 3 per cent per year since 1950.*
  *(Department for Transport, 2010b)*

*As you can see there has been a steady increase in the number of licensed vehicles between 1926 and 2009. With this information in mind, how might you expect the statistics for road fatalities to appear?*

*In 1979, road fatality figures were at a peak of 6,352, yet by 2008, they had dropped to 2,341 fatalities (Department for Transport, 2010a).*

*Why do you think this might be?*

*There are a number of factors which might influence these figures.*

- *An increase in safer design features in motor vehicles assists in protecting occupants in the event of an accident, for example, provision of seat belts, side impact bars, air bags, use of safety glass.*

- *There has been an increase in legislation to encourage safer driving, one of the more recent changes being the prohibition of use of hand-held mobile telephones when driving (Reg 110 Road Vehicles (Construction and Use) Regulations, 1986 (SI 1986/1078) and Road Traffic Act 1988, s.41D and Schedule 2 Road Traffic Offenders Act 1988).*

- *Speed restrictions have been increased; a lower limit of 20 mph being introduced in many built-up areas, and in recent years, government funding has led to increased placing of both mobile and static speed cameras to enable the detection of speeding offences as a means of deterring other drivers.*

- *It is important to recognise the long-term work conducted to educate drivers by the police and other agencies.*

---

*Figure 6.1 The figure demonstrates the strategic purpose for road policing. It is important to appreciate that policing targets are influenced at every level by information obtained from partner agencies and National Road Policing Forums.*

In keeping with response police officers, RPU officers are briefed at the commencement of each shift. Their role too is intelligence led. This concept has already been covered in Chapter 5. Officers are expected to know and understand the strategies and policing priorities set by their Tasking and Co-ordination Group, know local targets, gather information and intelligence and build relationships within the community.

The chart in Figure 6.1 above demonstrates the strategic purpose for road policing. It is important to appreciate that policing targets are influenced at every level by information obtained from partner agencies and National Road Policing forums.

You will recall that at the beginning of this chapter, it was stated that *the media often portrays police officers as driving everywhere at high speed, chasing and catching criminals*. Although this is not the main function of the RPU officer, there are occasions when it may become necessary. Clearly, this is a situation which can present risks if not carefully managed. Vehicle pursuits are not always planned; they will frequently be spontaneous as a result of an immediate situation.

A vehicle pursuit will usually be conducted in such a manner as to safely apprehend offenders and prevent crime. Officers involved in the pursuit of other vehicles are required to do so in accordance with clear guidelines issued by the Association of Chief Police Officers (ACPO, 2009a). RPU officers receive a higher level of driver training and are also trained in the use of appropriate tactics. Therefore, they will generally be the officers authorised to be involved in situations requiring the pursuit of a vehicle. One such tactic may be the deployment of a tyre-deflation system. Where a force has access to an Air Support Unit (ASU), they will be deployed to assist and are able to monitor the pursuit from above, enabling a greater distance between the pursuing vehicle and the subject vehicle, thus reducing risk.

Tactics will only be used where safe to do so. A pursuit will only be allowed to continue in accordance with the ACPO guidelines, and in the event of there being a perceived risk disproportionate to the situation, the pursuit will be discontinued.

Another means of preventing or controlling crime is through the lawful seizure of motor vehicles. A number of pieces of legislation incorporate powers of seizure by the police. Two such examples are shown below.

1. Where a driver is not believed to hold a valid driving licence, or the vehicle is being driven without insurance, the vehicle can be seized. Sections 164 and 165 of the Road Traffic Act 1988 (Retention and Disposal of Seized Motor Vehicles), Regulations 2005.

2. Where a vehicle is being driven inconsiderately or carelessly on a road, a constable must give the driver a warning, before seizing it under Section 59 of the Police Reform Act 2002.

As can be seen, the role of the RPU officer is varied. However, there are other roles within the RPU which are considered to support policing in other ways. Some of these will now be explored.

# The automated number plate recognition operator

This function is frequently located within the RPU. There are a number of associated roles linked to the operation of ANPR equipment and interpretation of its outcomes. Some roles are within the remit of a constable, whereas others may be conducted by non-sworn staff. These will be referred to later in this section. However, it is appropriate to consider the development of ANPR use first.

# Closed circuit television

Technology is advancing at a rapid pace. This section will begin by briefly looking at the CCTV and its development. It should be remembered that many other organisations and bodies also make use of CCTV, but here we will only consider its use by the police. The use of passive data from CCTV is now an established and generally accepted process aiding crime prevention and detection. Early police experimental CCTV was introduced in London and Liverpool in the 1960s. Further experiments were conducted during the 1970s and the1980s. The purpose of CCTV during the trials was explained variously as traffic control, watching over Parliament, preventing disorder during political demonstrations, protecting the public from violent attacks and also to reduce crime through psychologically attacking the criminal (Godfrey et al. 2008).

Larger scale trials were conducted in the 1990s, resulting in the publishing of the Home Office report 'CCTV: Looking Out for You' (Home Office, 1994). This in turn led to the 1999 Home Office crime reduction initiative prioritising funding to increase the availability of CCTV systems (Newburn, 2003). Today, CCTV systems are a common sight on housing estates, in town centres, in shops, protecting commercial premises, and in private homes. The CCTV is often effectively used to assist in the policing of communities.

Early CCTV systems had limited movement which enabled criminals to plan their crimes *out of range* of the camera or to plan a route which would enable them to avoid being seen on the camera. Today's camera systems are more sophisticated, cover a greater range and produce clearer images.

In terms of traffic management, CCTV cameras may be used to monitor traffic flow and identify congestion, and so forth. Many cameras used for this purpose are not actually used to record images. Those which are used for traffic-enforcement purposes such as monitoring junctions, parking restrictions and use of bus lanes tend to record images.

There is an ongoing discussion within the media around the use of surveillance cameras. It is suggested that the public cameras be divided into two groups – *bad* cameras being those which observe us as we go about our daily business and perhaps infringe our right to privacy, and *good* cameras which observe *them* (criminals) thereby preventing or aiding detection of crime (McCahill in Mason, 2003).

Interestingly in 2011, the estimated number of cameras in the country was recalculated at 1.85 million as opposed to earlier estimates of 4.2 million, suggesting that the average Briton is *caught on camera* up to 70 times per day rather than the 300 times previously estimated (BBC News, 2011).

This figure is representative of both CCTV and ANPR cameras. The next section will explain the use of the ANPR system further.

# Automated number plate recognition

The concept of CCTV has been taken a stage further. In 1976, the Police Scientific Development branch invented a process which has become known as Automatic Number Plate Recognition. This is based on CCTV, in that it is a camera system which automatically reads vehicle registration plates and takes a photograph. A fundamental difference is that the ANPR can access other data sources, compare the information on the registration plate against local and national electronic databases, interpret findings and return information immediately to the operator.

The benefit of this is that swift access to information enables the operator to act upon the outcome of the comparison without delay, which can then lead to actions being taken to disrupt, deter and detect criminal activity.

In 2003, the Home Office announced a national pilot of the ANPR scheme, involving 23 forces setting up 50 ANPR-enabled intercept teams (Coleman and McCahill, 2011). Today, all police forces have an ANPR capacity.

It has long been recognised that criminals do not restrict themselves to operating within their own force boundaries. Many use motor vehicles as their means of transport, and in doing so will cross those invisible boundary lines. This has been an underlying factor in the development of the strategic intent of the ANPR strategy for police forces, that is, to target criminals through their use of the road (ACPO, 2009b).

At the time of going to press, each force develops its own practice strategy in accordance with national guidelines; however, consultation taking place between March and May 2011 will lead to the development of a nationally agreed strategy for their use (Home Office, 2011).

ANPR would not be successful without a range of other people working in the background, administering and assessing the documentation and evidential material generated by this process. The practice guidance indicates recommended roles in the overall use of ANPR, some of which may be conducted by non-sworn staff.

- The ANPR manager who advises upon Force Strategy maintains auditing and QA processes and liaises with the national ANPR.

- The back office administrator who ensures that use is conducted in accordance with recommended practice.

- The controller who monitors ANPR hits, controls and co-ordinates the response.

- ANPR tactical advisers who will have a knowledge of investigative and evidential issues.

- Force data protection officers who ensure that use complies with the Data Protection Act.

- Intelligence staff who will access information produced by ANPR.

- Response or intercept officers who will respond to information and intercept subject vehicles.

- Investigators (police officers or police staff) who will use the ANPR data as part of their investigative roles.

(ACPO, 2009b)

It should be noted that these are only recommended roles. Forces may break down the responsibilities further or may appoint one person with responsibility for an amalgamation of the above. However, it does demonstrate the broad back office roles and reminds us that it is not always necessary for police officers to be engaged in all aspects of ANPR.

Perhaps the following example of the operational use of a mobile ANPR camera might demonstrate this further:

*A member of staff (non-sworn) will deploy an unmarked vehicle equipped with ANPR to monitor a specific area, for the purpose of policing general crime. The ANPR camera will gather information from vehicles which pass by, access relevant databases, e.g. Police National Computer and Driver and Vehicle Licensing Agency, interpreting that information. The person deploying the unit will relay the information gathered to a vehicle driven by a police constable, who will then intercept the subject vehicle and carry out relevant procedures.*

This is, of course, a simplified account, and other members of staff will be involved in any subsequent investigation. The above example would be considered to be an overt deployment. Most ANPR deployments are overt.

In the event of a covert deployment, specific legislation must be complied with – the Regulation of Investigatory Powers Act, 2000. An example of a covert deployment would be where the ANPR is used solely to identify an individual, for example, by deploying the ANPR on a route they are known to use at a time they are known to use it, and loading onto its database details of vehicles they are known to have access to. In this case, there would be a requirement to comply with the legislation by obtaining specific authority to conduct this deployment.

Fixed-site ANPR cameras have the capacity to operate 24 hours a day. Their exact locations are not generally publicised to prevent criminals using routes which bypass these sites and thereby prevent their movements from being recorded.

As can be seen, the ANPR may be used to gather intelligence which could be used as part of investigations. In this way, this information will contribute to intelligence-led policing.

# The road death/collision investigation unit officer

*Policing professional framework (Skills for Justice, 2011)*

**Road death/collision investigator**
To carry out this role you must be a competent detective constable.

**A road policing constable must be able to:**
• initiate investigations into road-related incidents.

**Personal qualities**
• Decision making.
• Leadership.
• Professionalism.
• Public service.
• Working with others.

All police constables are trained to investigate collisions. However, more serious collisions, and particularly road deaths, will be investigated by a specialist collision investigation officer, who has been trained to a higher level. This training will include in-depth vehicle examination, scene investigation and plan drawing. As you can see in the above table, the Policing Professional Framework (PPF) does define the skills required by the police officer conducting this role. However, this is a role which is not solely a police function, and some forces employ non-sworn officers to conduct some of the duties associated with collision investigation.

We have already briefly looked at some road death statistics within this chapter. In 2008, there was an average of seven deaths a day on Britain's roads (2,538). This is a markedly lower figure than in 1979 (6,352 fatalities) (Department for Transport, 2010).

REFLECTIVE TASK

*Read the following document.*

*Department for Transport (2010) Fatalities in Reported Road Accidents: 2008. Road Accident Statistics Factsheet No. 2 – 2010, available online at: www.dft.gov.uk/pgr/ statistics/datatablespublications/accidents/casualtiesgbar/suppletables factsheets/fatalities2008.pdf*

- *Who does it suggest are most likely to be victims of road death?*

- *Where does it suggest reported fatalities occur?*

- *Is there a particular day or days of the week when such incidents occur?*

- *What does the report suggest may be the cause of such incidents?*

It is an indication of the recognition of the seriousness of road-related deaths that in 2007, the ACPO developed practice advice to ensure that deaths on the road are professionally investigated. This is known as the Road Death Investigation Manual (ACPO, 2007a). It is based on the premise that all fatal collisions should be regarded as *unlawful killings* until the contrary is proved and that this will only be proved if thoroughly investigated.

The manual identifies a number of key roles, some of which may be conducted by non-sworn members of staff, and all of which will involve the collection and management of information essential to the investigation.

- The roads policing senior investigating officer (SIO). The SIO will be the lead investigator for the investigation. They will be selected and given additional training based on their knowledge and experience rather than rank.

- The collision investigator who will ensure the scene is secured to prevent the loss of evidence and conduct a thorough examination and associated investigations.

- The vehicle examiner who will establish the pre-collision mechanical condition of a vehicle and consider the likelihood of a vehicle-related condition having caused or contributed to the collision.

- The family liaison officer will be a single point of contact for a family of a victim and will offer guidance, pass on information and treat the family with sensitivity.

- The investigating officer will work with the SIO in gathering information relevant to the investigation, which will include obtaining statements from witnesses.

(ACPO, 2007b)

It is possible that two or more of these roles may be conducted by the same person.

As with any road collision, there are procedures that officers initially responding are required to conduct.

1. The initial assessment at the scene. This is conducted using a mnemonic (a memory aid) known as SAD CHALETS.

   - **S** – survey;

   - **A** – assess;

   - **D** – disseminate;

   - **C** – casualties – approximate numbers of dead, injured and uninjured;

   - **H** – hazards – for example, weather, spillages, location and dangers;

   - **A** – access – that is the best routes for emergency vehicles attending;

   - **L** – location – as accurate as possible;

   - **E** – emergency services – present and required;

   - **T** – type of incident – number of vehicles, buildings etc., involved;

   - **S** – safety – assessment of health and safety risks by those at the scene.

2. Making the scene safe and preserving life.

3. Preserving the scene.

4. Securing material and identifying witnesses.

5. identifying victims.

6. Identifying suspects.

(ACPO, 2007b)

There is no single chief cause for road collisions. Ignoring environmental factors, it is acknowledged that driver error, drink-driving, drug-driving, excess speed, use of hand-held mobile phones and driver fatigue can each be contributory factors (House of Commons Transport Committee, 2006). As has been shown earlier, many people are injured and die as a result of a collision. It is, therefore, essential that collisions are correctly investigated when they occur and also that preventative measures be taken in an attempt to reduce the risk of a collision. Such measures may include educating drivers or engineering out features in roads which may in some way contribute to collisions. The most effective approach to reducing collisions is a multi-agency approach, incorporating specialists from a range of agencies.

As we have been observing, even within the police service there are many different areas of working and many specialist roles. We will now look at the role of the firearms officer.

# The authorised firearms officer

*Policing professional framework (Skills for Justice, 2011)*

**Firearms officer/authorised firearms officer**
To carry out this role you must be a competent constable.

**An AFO must be able to:**
- contribute to the resolution of policing operations by providing a firearms capability.

**Personal qualities**
- Decision making.
- Leadership.
- Professionalism.
- Public service.
- Working with others.

The police are the only organisation, other than the military, whose officers are legally allowed to use force against members of the public while carrying out their duty (Rogers, 2003).

Waldren (2007) notes that Metropolitan Police records show 50 pairs of flintlock pocket pistols were purchased in 1829, the year the force was formed, and that by 1868, a supply of revolvers was kept at police stations. Officers were not routinely armed, however.

As early as the 1880s, the press was calling for the routine arming of police officers. This was the result of a scare about armed burglars, following the shooting of two police officers. In 1883, an official questionnaire sent to police officers canvassing their opinion revealed surprisingly that two-thirds of constables were keen to be armed. Although this was deemed to be not in keeping with the concept of police constables, a decision was taken to have a limited issue of firearms to those working in the most dangerous areas (Emsley, 2009).

Between about 1900 and 1925, Metropolitan Police officers openly carried firearms when guarding navy dockyards. These weapons were supplied by the Admiralty. However, in 1936, a change in regulations made it a requirement for constables to have a satisfactory reason before they would be issued with a firearm (Waldren, 2007).

During the Second World War, police officers again carried weapons to assist them in the protection of buildings and vulnerable points against saboteurs. Following the war, although most of the weapons were returned, the War Office agreed to a plan to store weapons at agreed points to enable access in the event of another war. Although this plan was never tested, it was discovered that the War Office had removed the weapons without informing police forces (Waldren, 2007).

Within the Metropolitan Police, officers continued to be armed if conducting protection duties; however, training in their use was very limited until 1966 when an incident involving the killing of three unarmed detectives occurred in the

Metropolitan Police area. This incident led to the introduction of a dedicated squad of firearms-trained constables, and the training of ten instructors (Rogers, 2003).

Since 1966, training has been developed and modified, often prompted by situations such as rioting in the 1980s, the deaths of Gail Kinshen, Stephen Waldorf, John Shorthouse and Cherry Groce and the general increase in the threat of terrorism.

Today, all firearms officers are trained in accordance with a national training package, although there are slight variations from force to force particularly where different weapons are used.

The firearms role is actually shown in the PPF as referring to two different roles, that of the firearms officer (FO) and that of the AFO (Skills for Justice, 2011). There is a distinction between the two in some force areas as is outlined in the following sections.

The FO is a constable trained in the use of firearms, but one who does not carry them at all times. He or she will not provide an immediate response to ongoing incidents, but may be drawn upon as an additional resource to support a pre-planned operation, or to assist another force in a mutual aid capacity.

The AFO will be armed routinely and will provide a spontaneous response to an ongoing firearms situation. In many forces, the AFO capacity will be integral to the RPU. This is partially because larger vehicles enable easier transportation of weapons. It is also because the broader area covered by the RPU means that an AFO is more likely to be available for swift deployment in the event of an incident.

It is essential that the use of any firearm or less-lethal weapon is in accordance with relevant legislation and also clear guidelines contained within the 'Manual of Guidance on the Management, Command and Deployment of Armed Officers' (ACPO/ACPOS, 2010). The 'Manual of Guidance' is a comprehensive document which outlines in detail the legal framework within which an FO must work, how weapons should be discharged, how they should be stored, issued and carried, how AFOs should be deployed, the relevant command structure and protocols and tactical guidance and post-deployment debriefing and welfare issues. The manual is the product of 180 years of policing in which a key principle has been that most police constables are not routinely armed. The arming of police constables is taken very seriously and, in collaboration with other organisations, clear rules have been established.

It is a requirement that firearms must only be used where there is no alternative, and the individual discharging a weapon must be able to justify their actions and believe that no alternative was possible without others being at risk of injury or loss of life. Use of force must always be proportionate to the risk involved (ACPO/ACPOS, 2010). In all cases, officers should always be mindful of their personal accountability for their own actions, and that their primary responsibility is to protect life.

A decision to discharge a weapon will be made by an individual on the basis of a visual assessment of the scene, knowledge of the wider operation, intelligence communicated and a direction from the commander.

Where possible *less lethal options* must be considered. These could include the following.

- Negotiation.

- Police dogs.

- Barriers to restrict or impede movement.

- Vehicle stopping devices.

- Tactics and devices designed to minimise risk to the subject.

- Tactical options set out in the ACPO 'Personal Safety Manual' and the ACPO 'Manual of Guidance on Keeping the Peace'.

(ACPO/ACPOS, 2010)

However, following trials, since July 2007, a new approach to arming officers has been taken, that of authorising AFOs in England and Wales to use a newly introduced less-lethal option – the taser – when facing violence or threats of violence (Joyce, 2011).

Tasers are hand-held electronic devices similar in shape to a handgun and are designed to fire two barbs, attached to the handset by thin wires, at an individual, with the intention of embedding the barbs in the clothing or superficial skin on the torso and/or lower limb. The wires then transmit short-duration, high-voltage and low-current pulses when actuated. This has the effect of inducing a temporary disruption of voluntary muscle control and intense pain, which incapacitates the person (ACPO, 2008).

It was announced in July 2007 that a 12-month trial would take place in ten police forces enabling deployment of the taser by specially trained units other than firearms officers.

Figures for the use of the taser by armed officers between 20 July 2007 and 30 June 2009 indicate that in England and Wales it was used a total of 1,968 times by armed officers. The definition of *used* is extremely broad and includes simply drawing the weapon (187 times) and aiming it without discharging it (81 times). During the period September 2007 and June 2009 in the ten participating police forces, there were 1,267 uses by the specially trained units, of which the weapon was simply drawn on 261 occasions and aimed on 62 occasions (Home Office, 2009).

The 12-month trial was considered successful, and in December 2008, the home secretary agreed to allow chief officers to extend the use of the taser to specially trained units in situations whereby they would be facing violence or threats of violence of a severe nature. In order to facilitate this, eight million pounds was provided by the Home Office to enable the purchase and distribution of 7,000 tasers. The use of tasers is very closely regulated and monitored.

The taser is only one of the less-lethal options and those listed earlier should not be overlooked as successful in many instances.

# C H A P T E R   S U M M A R Y

In this chapter, we have briefly looked at a number of roles linked to the work of the RPU, such as the challenging roles of the RPU officer, the ANPR operator and the road death/collision investigator. Additionally, we have explored the specialist, and often misunderstood role, of the AFO. Some of these roles may be conducted by police officers and some others by members of the police staff (civilians). Each of these plays an essential role, as part of a highly trained team, in the process of dealing with crime and road-related incidents.

## CASE STUDY

*Earlier in this chapter, reference was made to CCTV camera evidence. In Chapter 3, we found out that CCTV cameras were present in the shop itself. From witness evidence, we have a physical description of two men and the clothing they are wearing. CCTV footage will be viewed to confirm the witness information, and the local intelligence unit are analysing information.*

*An officer has been despatched to the CCTV camera suite located on the outskirts of the town centre. From viewing street CCTV camera evidence, more information is gathered. It is possible to see two males walking into the Newsagents, then reappearing a brief time later, and to see them running away from the Newsagents, disappearing from view as they approach the town-centre mall. The mall is a privately owned area, so CCTV cameras are not monitored in this suite; however, all external cameras in the locality are examined.*

*The two men are next seen running past a camera located in an adjoining road. They approach a parked motor vehicle, apparently a Ford Focus, and jump into it. Initially, the registration number of the vehicle is not visible; however, it appears to be a Ford Focus.*

*The motor vehicle is then seen to drive off away from the camera. It is possible to see its registration number, which is TU10 XXX. Further investigation shows that this vehicle has been driven along nearby roads immediately after the incident. The officer attending the scene passes the confirmed registration number back to the control room and the information he has found from the cameras, and takes steps to secure the recordings for later use as evidence.*

*Control room staff alert other officers, including the AFOs, of the confirmed make and number of the vehicle. They also ensure the registration number has been passed to the back office administrator who inputs the details into the ANPR system. This process takes only seconds and enables a historical check of previous movements of the vehicle together with an ongoing check outlining any points at which the suspect vehicle passes the camera.*

*The control room have already alerted an on-call firearms tactical adviser, who is assessing any information relating to the suspect vehicle and its occupants. As each new piece of information is received, they will adjust their instructions to the AFOs allocated to the incident.*

*Very quickly the back office administrator begins to receive information from ANPR cameras around the local area and is able to show the route the suspect vehicle took to approach the town centre, and also begins to receive information as to its route away from the centre. This information is relayed to the tactical adviser who directs vehicles to strategic points on the anticipated route including Southlands Road, which has been identified by the local intelligence unit. The ASU is also alerted and asked to attend the area.*

*The manner in which the vehicle is stopped will vary in accordance with the information known about it and the quality of that information. Attempting to stop the vehicle might lead to a vehicle pursuit, or it might lead to the discharging of firearms. At all times, officers will be conscious of the advice of the tactical adviser and aware of their own safety, avoiding putting this at risk. The ASU will view the vehicle from the air, recording its route and sending a live video link to the control room to enable maximum information to be relayed to those controlling the sequence of events.*

*When the suspect vehicle, TU10 XXX, was finally safely stopped by the RPU in conjunction with the AFOs, checks were conducted to ensure the safety of the police officers present. This included the occupants being searched to ensure they were not concealing weapons (such as a firearm or knife), and steps were taken to ensure that the correct vehicle had been stopped. The two suspects were cautioned and arrested on suspicion of robbery and placed in a police vehicle for transporting to the nearest custody suite. The suspect vehicle was seized by the police for later examination by crime-scene investigators. No firearm was recovered.*

# Self-assessment questions

1. When was the first police vehicle introduced and how was it known?

2. Give an example of a decriminalised offence.

3. Name some of the activities that RPU officers will engage in as a means of achieving their goal of casualty reduction.

4. Which guidelines should be adhered to in the event of a vehicle pursuit?

5. What do the acronyms CCTV and ANPR relate to?

6. Why are locations of fixed-site ANPR cameras not generally publicised?

7. What do the individual letters of the mnemonic SAD CHALETS refer to?

8. Which role referred to in this chapter offers families of victims a single point of contact for information?

9. List some of the causes of road collisions.

10. List examples of *less lethal options* which may be an alternative to the use of a firearm.

REFERENCES

ACPO (2007a) *Practice Advice on the Policing of Roads.* Wyboston: NPIA.

ACPO (2007b) *Road Death Investigation Manual.* Wyboston: NPIA.

ACPO (2008) *Operational Use of Taser by Authorised Firearms Officers.* London: ACPO.

ACPO (2009a) *The Management of Police Pursuits Guidance.* London: ACPO.

ACPO (2009b) *Practice Advice on the Management and Use of Automatic Number Plate Recognition.* Wyboston: NPIA.

ACPO /ACPOS (2009) *Police Driving Manual 2009.* London: ACPO.

ACPO/ACPOS (2010) *The Manual of Guidance on the Management, Command and Deployment of Armed Officers*, 2nd edition. Wyboston: NPIA.

Arden, M R, Fletcher, E and Taylor, C (2008) *Metropolitan Police Images: 1: Motor Vehicles.* Chichester: Phillimore.

BBC News (2011) *CCTV Camera Estimates Halved by Police.* Available online at: www.bbc.co.uk/news/uk-12641568 (accessed 3 March 2011).

Cleveland Police (2010) *Report of the Chief Constable to the Chair and Members of the Operational Policing Panel: Speed Awareness Course Update. 22 January 2010.* Available online at www.clevelandpa.org.uk/admin/uploads/attachment/22_January_2010-Speed%20Awareness%20Course%20Update.pdf (accessed 26 February 2011).

Coleman, R and McCahill, M (2011) *Surveillance and Crime.* London: Sage.

Corbett, C (2003) *Car Crime.* Cullompton: Willan.

Department for Transport (2010a) *Fatalities in Reported Road Accidents: 2008.* Road Accident Statistics Factsheet No. 2 – 2010. Available online at www.dft.gov.uk/pgr/statistics/datatablespublications/accidents/casualtiesgbar/suppletablesfactsheets/fatalities2008.pdf (accessed 26 February 2011).

Department for Transport (2010b) *Transport Statistics Great Britain: 2010.* Available online at www.dft.gov.uk/pgr/statistics/datatablespublications/tsgb/latest/tsgb2010vehicles.pdf (accessed 26. February 2011).

Dix, M C and Layzell, A D (1983) *Road Users and the Police.* Kent: Croom Helm.

Elliott, M and Broughton, J (2005) *How Methods and Levels of Policing Affect Road Casualty Rates.* Transport and Road Research Laboratory, TRL 637.

Emsley, C (1993) 'Mother, What Did Policemen Do When There Weren't Any Motors?' The Law, the Police and the Regulation of Motor Traffic in England, 1900–1939. *The Historical Journal*, 36: 357–81.

Emsley, C (2009) *The Great British Bobby: A History of British Policing from the 18th Century to the Present*. London: Quercus.

Godfrey, B S, Lawrence, P and Williams, C A (2008) *History and Crime*, London: Sage.

Griffiths, R, Davies, R F, Henderson, R and Sheppard, D (1980) *Incidence and Effects of Police Action on Motoring Offences as Described by Drivers*. Transport & Road Research Laboratory, Supplementary Report 543.

Hardwick P, Cleveland Police, Road Policing Unit. March 2011. Personal Communication.

Hicks, J and Allen, G (1999) *A Century of Change: Trends in UK Statistics Since 1900*. House of Commons Research Paper 99/111. London: House of Commons.

Home Office (1994) *CCTV: Looking Out for You*. London: Home Office.

Home Office (2009) *Figures on the Reported and Recorded Uses of Taser by Police Forces in England and Wales*. Available online at tna.europarchive.org/20100419081706/http://scienceandresearch.homeoffice.gov.uk/images/106966/PTaser_figs_Nov_09.pdf (accessed 2 March 2011).

Home Office (2010) *Operational Policing: Road Traffic*. Available online at tna.europarchive.org/20100419081706/http://www.police.homeoffice.gov.uk/op (accessed 22 February 2011).

Home Office (2011) *Consultation on a Code of Practice Relating to Surveillance Cameras*. Available online at www.homeoffice.gov.uk/publications/consultations/cons-2011-cctv/code-surveillance-cameras?view=Binary (accessed 2 March 2011).

House of Commons Transport Committee (2006) *Roads Policing and Technology: Getting the Right Balance*. 10th Report of Session 2005/06. London: The Stationery Office.

James, L and Nahl, D (2000) *Road Rage and Aggressive Driving: Steering Clear of Highway Warfare*. Amherst: Prometheus.

Joyce, P (2011) *Policing: Development & Contemporary Practice*. London: Sage.

Mason, P (2003) *Criminal Visions: Media Representations of Crime and Justice*. Cullompton: Willan.

Metropolitan Police Service (n.d.) *History of the Metropolitan Police: Black Marias*. Available online at www.met.police.uk/history/black_marias.htm (accessed 22 February 2011).

Newburn, T (ed) (2003) *Handbook of Policing*. Cullompton: Willan.

Richards, D, Cookson, R, Smith, S, Ganu, V and Pittman, N (2010) *The Characteristics of Speed Related Collisions*. Road Safety Research Report No 117. London: Department for Transport.

Richards, D C (2010) *Relationship between Speed and Risk of Fatal Injury: Pedestrians and Car Occupants*. Road Safety Web Publication 17. London: Department for Transport.

Rogers, C and Lewis, R (2007) *Introduction to Police Work*. Cullompton: Willan.

Rogers, M D (2003) 'Police Force! An Examination of the Use of Force, Firearms and Less-Lethal Weapons by British Police'. *The Police Journal*, 76(3): 189–203.

Rowe, M (2008) *Introduction to Policing*. London: Sage.

Sheldon, B, and Wright, P (2010) *Policing and Technology*. Exeter: Learning Matters.

Skills for Justice (2011) *Policing Professional Framework*. Available online at www. skillsforjustice-ppf.com (accessed 24 February 2011).

Stead, P J (1985) *The Police of Britain*. London: Macmillan.

Stephenson, C, Wicks, J, Elliot, M and Thomson, J (2010) *Monitoring Speed Awareness Courses: Baseline Data Collection*. Road Safety Research Report No 115. London: Department for Transport.

Waldren, M J (2007) *Armed Police: The Police Use of Firearms Since 1945*. Stroud: Sutton.

*USEFUL WEBSITES*

www.acpo.police.uk/ (Association of Chief Police Officers).

www.dft.gov.uk/help/findinginfo (Department for Transport).

www.homeoffice.gov.uk/ (Home Office).

www.itai.org/links.asp (Institute of Traffic Accident Investigators).

www.npia.police.uk (National Policing Improvement Agency).

www.trl.co.uk/about_trl/ (Transport Research Laboratory (TRL)).

*LEGISLATION*

Police Reform Act, 2002.

Regulation of Investigatory Powers Act, 2000.

Road Vehicles (Construction and Use) Regulations, 1986.

Road Traffic Act, 1988.

Road Traffic Act, 1988 (Retention and Disposal of Seized Motor Vehicles) Regulations 2005.

Road Traffic Offenders Act, 1988.

# 7 The custody suite

PETER WILLIAMS

**CHAPTER OBJECTIVES**

By the end of this chapter you will have:

- understood key elements surrounding the historical development of the police custody role;
- understood the role of the custody officer;
- understood the role of the detention officer;
- understood the role of the case management officer;
- gained an understanding of the overall function of the custody suite;
- identified key issues in relation to detainees at risk of self-harm/suicide.

## Introduction

This chapter explores the functions of those who deal with individuals following their detention by the police.

- Custody officer.

- Lay visitors (or custody visitors).

- Detention officer/custody assistant.

- Case management officer.

The chapter examines the role and function of police officers and support staff in relation to the detention of prisoners by the police. That sentence itself represents a massive understatement as to the controversy that has been witnessed in relation to police detention *per se*, particularly over the past 40 years.

To fully appreciate the crucial and pivotal role played by the custody officer in any police investigation, supported by his/her colleagues in the custody suite, a historical analysis is required which highlights several of the keynote events that have culminated in the enhanced professionalism incumbent upon the custody officer, within the contemporary police service. If the role is undertaken properly, it can be one of the most interesting and rewarding, although often grossly underestimated and unvalued, within the service.

Do it right and the custody officer will gain the respect of all – colleagues within the custody environment, senior officers, arresting officers, civilian escort person-nel contracted to private companies, medical professionals, solicitors and their representatives and even the prisoners themselves. Custody suites can be excep-tionally intimidating and lonely places particularly for the first-time detainee, as we shall illustrate later in the chapter. Prisoners need to have confidence that the person in charge of the suite and the staff within it will do the right thing consist-ently when and if required.

However, do it wrong and the custody officer will not only lose respect, but also potentially put serious cases of crime at risk of being formally dismissed at court and leave the chief constable open to future civil litigation, in addition to potential disciplinary action directed at the custody officer himself or herself. It can often appear an invidious role to some; however, if conducted professionally, untoward incidents can be kept to an absolute minimum.

The police have been responsible for 'housing' detained prisoners well before the inception of Peel's 'new police' who first ventured onto the streets at 6 p.m. on 30 September 1829 in London and have therefore acted as custodians for centuries.

For example, within the city of Liverpool, two rather odd-looking stone struc-tures were erected in 1787 in the Everton area and in 1796 in the Wavertree area which, at first appearance, resemble smaller versions of the Leaning Tower of Pisa. Originally designed as a lock-up for drunken prisoners and the responsibility of the local village constable, they remain a tangible legacy to a very early and primary police function (Williams, 2005).

In relation to our case study of the robbery at 'Roman's Newsagent, High Street', the first knowledge that the custody staff are likely to have will be a telephone call from the control room enquiring if the custody suite can accept persons who have been arrested for the offence. In itself it appears a straightforward request. However, like any other establishment that offers accommodation, the custody suite can and often does become full to capacity where there are 'no vacancies'. The difference being that there are strict rules and guidance as to the detention of persons, unlike paying guests. This in itself is due to the historical legacy that has evolved over the post-war period to which we now turn.

# Historical development

The role of the custody officer is a very modern creation, formally established by the Police and Criminal Evidence (PACE) Act, 1984, which became effective from 1 January 1986. This placed the role on a statutory footing. It is normally per-formed by an officer in the rank of sergeant, but in expedient circumstances, any officer can undertake the role. In practical terms, this rarely happens and if it does it would only be in rural areas where a detainee was being held for a short period of time, for example, to facilitate a charging process. Within a conventional operational setting, however, it is usually a sergeant based at a custody suite that operates 24/7 and provides operational support to front-line police officers, such as those response officers responding to 'Roman's Newsagents'.

One of the main justifications for the creation of the role of custody officer was as a result of the Royal Commission into Criminal Procedure (RCCP), 1981, chaired by Sir Cyril Phillips, vice chancellor of London University. This was the main vehicle that laid the foundation for the introduction of PACE, 1984, as Chapter 4 has already indicated. The RCCP wished to see a separation of powers between that of the investigation and that of the prosecution. As a result, the Prosecution of Offenders Act, 1985, was enacted and the independent Crown Prosecution Service (CPS) was introduced. Prior to that, the police forces, that is, the investigators, instructed their own prosecuting bodies and the RCCP clearly wished to create a clear demarcation of boundaries. This sentiment expressed by the RCCP led to one of the primary functions of the custody officer – although a police officer, they remain 'independent' of any investigation and therefore play no part in it.

This is often a difficult position to reconcile to. The custody officer is a police officer, normally a sergeant, a full member of the investigating police service, who wears the same uniform and to the outsider is very much part of that machinery.

However, this is where the professionalism of the individual comes into play. At all times the custody officer must remain outside the investigation process, irrespective of the rank and status of the senior investigating officer, and fulfil the role as the Act envisaged and in a manner in which that professionalism is acknowledged and respected.

Prior to the RCCP, semi-formal arrangements existed in respect to police custody. The British police service is based on a constabulary-style structure, which broadly reflects the county boundaries that evolved in respect of local public administration. Therefore, police forces have been either disbanded or forced to merge since the introduction of the 'new police' in 1829 to mirror that. Anomalies still exist, and it remains very much a local arrangement, particularly when compared to other EU countries such as France, which has both a national civilian police service and a gendarmerie. Consequently, there was little central direction in operational matters, and individual police forces developed their own systems.

Furthermore, most police stations were built with a cell area for detaining prisoners, normally no more than about four to six cells, unlike the custody-suite complexes that are familiar nowadays, housing on an average about 20 individual cells. Many are even larger than that.

Liverpool City Police, later Merseyside Police, which was created as a result of the force amalgamations and mergers referred to earlier, operated a role known as a 'Bridewell sergeant', a position with distinct parallels with that of the contemporary custody officer.

Although the duties of the Bridewell sergeants were not solely devoted to the detention of prisoners as that of the modern-day custody officer, they were responsible for that function. In quieter periods, the Bridewell sergeant was also expected to deal with routine callers at the police station front counter, record the details of driving documents being produced, receive the numerous 'lost' dogs that well-meaning people and concerned children consistently brought to police stations, and receive incoming telephone calls and resolve the enquiries associated with them. Almost a jack of all trades in relation to daily police station life.

The role, therefore, was somewhat blurred and no specific training in respect of the bridewell element was provided apart from the fact that the Bridewell sergeant had assumed greater knowledge of criminal law, by being successful in the annual sergeants examination and subsequently being promoted by the chief constable. The arresting officers, normally police officers, brought prisoners to the bridewell area of the police station for detention and subsequent processing. Furthermore, the role was often rotated with that of other operational commitments, such as patrol duties. This provides further evidence of the jack-of-all-trades approach, a situation that surprisingly exists in some areas even today.

The cell areas of police stations in Liverpool were referred to officially and also within day-to-day police jargon as 'the bridewell', signifying an area of a police station that retained special status.

However, one such area was referred to as the 'Main Bridewell'. This was situated alongside Liverpool City Magistrates Court and housed prisoners awaiting court appearances, or those following court appearances, collection for HM Prison, either on remand or having been convicted. The history and operational functions of the Main Bridewell provide some interesting insights into the historical development of the custody officer. Moreover, it is worth noting that this building was completed in 1860, some 30 years after the arrival of the new police, and perhaps unbelievably, remained operational as a police responsibility and as a fully operational custody unit, until as recently as 2000.

---

### REFLECTIVE TASK

*Go to the following website and after having read the contents, answer the questions below.*

*www.britishlistedbuildings.co.uk/en-213886-main-bridewell-liverpool*

- *What was the 'Main Bridewell' originally designed as?*

- *In 1860 how many cells did it have?*

- *What was this reduced to?*

- *Under 'reasons for designation', what was it about that it was able to 'successfully convey'?*

*Having read the description of the building and the reasons for its designation as a Listed Building, consider the following.*

*If you had been arrested by the police for the first time and were taken to the Main Bridewell, what would your initial feelings and thoughts be?*

*If your answer to the above question included the word 'anxious' or something similar, what would you attempt to do about it?*

The Metropolitan Police also had a very similar arrangement to that of the Bridewell sergeant through the position of station sergeant – a rank which has now been abolished, but sat between sergeant and inspector within the uniform rank structure. In fact, the last station police sergeant in the Metropolitan Police, William Palmer, retired in January 1980 (www.fomphc.org.uk/) and following this the rank effectively disappeared, perhaps somewhat myopically given what was being considered by RCCP at that time and what later transpired under PACE. It must be stressed that a station sergeant's duties were diverse and largely supervisory, not exclusively designated to the processing of prisoners. However, the significant point here is that there was recognition within the United Kingdom's largest police force that there was a role for somebody of that rank to oversee what was occurring operationally within the police station.

Again, like those duties of the Merseyside Police Bridewell sergeant, there are clear similarities with that of the custody officer, the fundamental difference being that the role of custody officer was effectively codified as a result of PACE – an aspect that will become apparent as this chapter unfolds.

Other police forces had far less formal arrangements, and sergeants effectively only 'accepted the charge' or in layman's terms, listened to the reasons for the arrest from the arresting officers, opened a charge sheet and later formally charged and bailed prisoners. The actual responsibility of care towards the detainee was performed by the station constable, who not surprisingly had other duties and on occasions could findthe workload rather challenging. Under those arrangements, the actual *accountability* in respect of the welfare of the prisoners was rather unclear, an issue which PACE has now clarified.

## The contemporary role of the custody officer

The role of the custody officer has clear comparisons with the roles of both the Bridewell sergeant and the station sergeant, the fundamental difference being that the role of custody officer is now placed on a statutory footing, through PACE. Consequently, it is universally accepted that the duties are both wide and diverse. However, there are duties that a custody officer must do as required by statute, and we will now focus on some of them.

The oft-quoted statement 'assisting the police with their enquiries' never really existed in law and certainly does not ever since the introduction of PACE and the associated Codes of Practice, to which Code 'C' specifically applies to custody issues.

Arrested persons must be brought directly to a custody officer in order to get their detention authorised. Although reasons for the arrest and reasons for detention are obviously closely linked, they are different issues which some people have difficulty in appreciating. For example, the offence of burglary like most other offences nowadays provides a power of arrest. However, there are three potential reasons in law why an arrested person can be detained in the custody suite.

1. In order to secure or preserve evidence.

2. To obtain evidence by questioning.

3. To be charged with an offence.

It is the role of the custody officer to listen to the circumstances of the arrest from the arresting officer and consider if there are reasonable grounds for detention based on one or more of the criteria above. However, if the custody officer is not convinced that there are reasonable grounds for detention, the charge can be 'refused' and the arrested person released immediately. This course of action occurs more than perhaps is first thought.

Assuming that threshold has been reached, detention is authorised by the custody officer for a period of six hours, to a point which is known as the 'first review' – six hours hence from the time that detention was first authorised. Subsequent periodic reviews at the six hourly and 15 hourly stages are by an inspector until 24 hours is reached. Normally, most prisoners have been dealt with by this stage, but on occasions, a superintendent can authorise detention up to a period of 36 hours. Further detention until 96 hours can only be granted by a magistrate's court.

---

REFLECTIVE TASK

*At about 0910 hours on a weekday morning, a female clerical worker situated in a first floor office sees a white male, aged about 20–25 years force the patio doors at the rear of a nearby dwelling, that the office block overlooked, enter the house and emerge about 90 seconds later with a flat-screen television. The male then goes from the rear to the front of the property, and the female loses sight of him. She contacts 999 believing that the property has been forcibly entered and property stolen and speaks to a call handler.*

*Some minutes later at about 0920 hours, a police officer in a response vehicle, who has heard the original call, sees a male of a similar description running along a road situated about 500 yards from the premises that were attacked. The police officer speaks to the male, who is heavily out of breath and panting, and ascertains that he is running for a bus in order to attend the local Magistrate's court on time, in order to answer a charge of handling stolen goods. The police officer is unhappy with the explanation, but it is confirmed via radio that the male is on bail for handling stolen goods and is due in court that morning.*

*While he is speaking to the male, another call is received from a nearby house-holder to say that somebody has just thrown a flat-screen television into his front garden and run off in the direction where the police officer is talking to the male. A description of any person seen at this location is not obtained by the call handler. This property is situated about 250 yards away.*

*With this latest information, the officer arrests the male on suspicion of burglary, and the male is transported to the nearest custody suite where the circumstances of the arrest are explained to you, the custody officer.*

- *Would you authorise detention for this male given that on being searched at the custody office he has in his possession an inhaler for an asthma problem?*

*You also learn during the reception/booking-in procedure that the original female caller has subsequently left her office by taxi in order to catch a train to London for an early-afternoon business meeting. Furthermore, the second caller who reported the television set in the front garden is of the view that the male who dumped the property in his front garden was a black male, but cannot describe him further. A constable who has attended the scene of crime has just reported that a cigarette has been recently discarded just outside the patio doors and although the arrested male has cigarettes in his possession, they are a different brand from that found at the scene.*

- *Would you authorise detention for this male given that on being searched at the custody office he has in his possession an inhaler for an asthma problem? Remember, as the custody officer, you play no part in the investigation whatsoever.*

- *If you have authorised detention for this arrested male, for which of the three criteria outlined above will he be detained?*

- *List your reasons for either doing so or not doing so and 'refusing' the charge.*

- *To assist you to arrive at your decision, because it is yours and yours alone, consider the following.*

*Is there sufficient evidence to charge this male with the offence of burglary?*

*If not, what other opportunities to seek any further evidence are there? Fingerprints, forensic (saliva), identification parade, formal interview?*

*However, if you feel that reasonable grounds do not exist, you should refuse the charge. In those circumstances, a further requirement of the custody officer would be to complete an internal report explaining the reasons why the 'charge was refused'.*

If the male above was accepted into custody, the next function of the custody officer would be to open a custody record. This is a written record of a prisoner's time at the custody suite from initial reception to either release on bail, or transfer to court or another custody suite, that is, when the detained person leaves the custody suite.

The function of a custody record, and in today's world most are actually completed through a computer terminal linked to the force-information technology system, is comparable to an in-patient record normally kept at the end of a hospital bed. On that document which we are all familiar with, a patient's 'observations' are recorded. The same applies to a police custody record. Prior to PACE, the only comparable documentation was not anywhere as detailed and was known as a 'charge sheet'. Other information pertaining to the prisoner, but not directly associated with the offence for which the arrest was made or the individual's personal details, such as meals provided, was briefly recorded in the station memo book. This system allowed other occurrences within the station to be recorded, along with information such as the contents of the police station safe. A designated document where relevant material directly connected to the custody of the prisoner rarely existed, if ever.

The custody record changed that situation, although virtually all are now electronic documents, and a number of forces in the United Kingdom have their new custody and case-preparation systems supplied by either the National Strategy for Police Information Systems (NSPIS) or a Canadian-based software company which supplies a system called Niche Technology Records Management Systems (Niche RMS) (Police Product Review, February/March, 2011, p 6). The fact that there is not one uniform system is reflective of the Constabulary-style structure of police forces within the United Kingdom, although it should be noted that some of the larger forces in the country, including West Yorkshire, Merseyside, Cleveland and Hampshire, have chosen to implement Niche RMS.

The station memo book would have been a key tool for either the Bridewell or station sergeant but not the contemporary custody officer who is accountable for the care and welfare of the prisoners. This includes the safe storage of their personal property and therefore needs detailed recording, as opposed to cursory updates that was the accepted practice with the station memo book.

In relation to the accountability of the custody officer in respect of care and welfare, a key function which is required by law to be performed is the formal notification of rights according to the PACE Act, 1984. This is normally carried out at the time of booking-in and further illustrates the significance of the independent role of the contemporary custody officer. It is difficult to envisage the detective in charge of the case being responsible for this task. If that were the case, it would no doubt become the first issue of contention in any subsequent contested criminal trial. No doubt the RCCP considered that point when the overall role of the custody officer was under consideration. Therefore, at this point the custody officer is required to inform the arrested person of three things and provide a written notice to that effect. Foreign language versions are, or should be, readily available. An arrested person is:

1. entitled to have somebody informed about his whereabouts;

2. entitled to free legal advice and consultation with a solicitor either in person or via the telephone;

3. entitled to see a copy of the Codes of Practice.

On the custody record itself, the detainee endorses in writing that the notice has been served and also indicates the preferences as to any requirement for a solicitor. Furthermore, the custody record lists details of cash and other valuable property removed from the prisoner, other personal property removed and the reasons for that, that is, to prevent harm.

During a prisoner's detention, it also records details such as drinks and meals taken, routine visits by the detention officers, when taken and returned from interviews with the investigation officers and if seen and when by a forensic medical examiner (FME) or a medical practitioner. Once completed the next task is to place the detainee in a cell, and unlike other jurisdictions, in the United Kingdom, multi-occupancy is only permitted in the most exceptional circumstances, and the recommended practice is one person per cell.

However, this is often an opportunity for teamwork between the custody officer and the detention officer to come into play. Prior to placing the prisoner in the cell, the individual's details need to be input into the Police National Computer (PNC), not merely to obtain details of any previous convictions or offences currently outstanding, but to ascertain if there are 'warning signals' held on the PNC, such as 'mental disorder', 'self-harm' or in respect of safety of the custody staff, 'violent'.

In relation to the first warning signal, 'mental disorder', if you return to Chapter 4 and re-read the miscarriage of justice in relation to Judith Ward, you can see how the issue of mental illness was instrumental in this miscarriage. It is also a good illustration of why the custody officer should remain independent of the investigation and what the legislation was trying to achieve by identifying the status of investigation and prosecution as being separate and distinct. Issues such as these can clearly affect a detainee's detention at the custody suite, and key information that the custody staff need to be aware of before the prisoner is placed in a cell. In practical terms, particularly during busy periods, this is easier said than done, but can make the difference between an untoward incident occurring or not occurring. Being proactive is a key professional trait in a custody environment and can keep unwelcome incidents to an absolute minimum. Sitting back ready to react only if something does happen will guarantee only one thing – something will happen.

At this juncture, it is prudent to take some time to reflect on what has occurred over the past 40 years in particular and how this is being addressed by modern-day custody staff.

# Prevention of deliberate self-harm and suicide

It is so easy to underestimate the significance of this area, not merely to an individual prisoner and their families, but to the credibility of the police service as a whole. It is worth looking back at some key events that occurred that illustrate this very issue.

*The circumstances of the above case underline the issues that were undermining public confidence at that time regarding the safety of persons in police custody in particular and also the police service as a whole in respect of credibility. On this latter point, as Chapter 4 has indicated, the harbinger for the RCCP was the 1977 Fisher Report. However, within the wider criminal justice system, two other issues were also causing public concern. The first was the enforcement of the so-called sus laws and the second was the police treatment of suspects in custody, hence, the significance of the Towers case in this regard.*

*Go to the website provided below, which is a record of Hansard. It is about this case being raised in the House of Commons. The debate is opened by Mr Giles Radice who also outlines the circumstances of the incident.*

*http://hansard.millbanksystems.com/commons/1977/dec/12/mr-liddle-towers*

- *What previous convictions did Liddle Towers have?*

- *Who, according to Mr Radice, is responsible for the injuries to Liddle Towers?*

- *Who supports Liddle Towers's account of the events?*

- *What is being brought 'into disrepute in a more general way'?*

- *According to David Watkins, where is the 'major concern' manifesting itself?*

- *Mr Eldon Griffiths states that a film was broadcast that very week depicting violence by whom?*

- *From this written account of the parliamentary debate and your reflections on the earlier task regarding the Main Bridewell, list what you feel are the issues that the police service needed to address in respect of detained persons in police custody.*

Clearly, there is widespread concern that gratuitous violence was being perpetrated by police officers and this disquiet was aggravated by the apparent lack of accountability, which the Hansard debate indicates.

Around the time that the RCCP was reporting in 1981, Britain witnessed some of the worst rioting in modern times, initially in Brixton, London, in April 1981 and later on that summer in Toxteth, Liverpool (Blake et al., 2010, pp 128–30). As a result of these disturbances, the then home secretary ordered a formal enquiry led by Lord Scarman, who subsequently published his report later that year. In it, he recommended that independent persons should be appointed by police authorities to monitor the treatment of persons in police custody. This idea was taken up by the Government, and 'Lay Visitors' were introduced, initially as a pilot in 1983. Subsequently, the scheme has flourished, and lay visitors are now known as custody visitors in most forces.

---

### REFLECTIVE TASK

*Lay visitors or custody visitors*

*Go to the following website and complete the following tasks.*

*www.mpa.gov.uk/committees/x-cdo/2000/000926/14/*

*Read through this report from the Metropolitan Police Authority and answer the following.*

- *How many forces were involved in the initial pilot scheme?*

- *What is the 'overall objective' of lay visiting?*

- *What do you see as the primary role of lay visitors?*

- *On a routine single visit to a police station, normally how many lay visitors are there?*

- *When was the National Association for Lay Visiting established?*

---

Custody staff should have nothing to fear from custody visitors who if handled professionally can become major allies of custody staff for several reasons.

First, it is natural for anybody to feel somewhat aggrieved that complete strangers can have almost unrestricted access to custody suites in order to scrutinise and comment upon, in writing, the work of the staff and the general condition of the custody suite. Consequently, on occasion, on a personal level, ill-feeling may arise. However, custody staff are professionals and therefore have an obligation to deal with all the people within the custody suite in the correct manner, as the introductory section to this chapter suggests. Furthermore, custody staff must remember that in terms of professional knowledge, they have the distinct advantage as independent custody visitors are what their original title states they are – lay visitors. In many circumstances, they rely totally on the staff for advice and clarification, albeit some of the longer standing custody visitors have developed a good working knowledge of legislation and procedures. In the occasional event of encountering overzealous custody visitors, they are almost certainly without exception invited to resign immediately. Police authorities and the custody visitors themselves take this role with utmost seriousness, particularly the conduct of the appointed visitors, and are not there in any supervisory capacity.

Second, in respect of vulnerable prisoners such as those at risk of self-harm or suicide, many custody visitors have a professional background in disciplines such as nursing, social work, the clergy and/or all-round life skills. Many possess soft skills which can identify detainees at risk a lot sooner than the custody staff and can prove to be a very useful resource in that regard. Moreover, most custody environments are subject to digital video and audio recordings, and since this innovation, there has been an argument proffered that the role of the independent custody visitor is now somewhat mitigated. What must be remembered, though, is that custody visitors speak directly to prisoners in situ within the custody suite, whereas cameras do not.

Third, most visits occur during the evening which is traditionally the busiest period for the custody staff. As a consequence, custody visitors witness the pressures placed upon custody staff first hand, as opposed to some police managers who merely review the monthly performance data and see little of the operational interface. Besides, custody visitors identify issues within the suite that require attention, as do the custody staff who work there. This often requires sanction from a tier of management within the force that is removed from the operational day-to-day routines of the custody suite and does not appreciate how the problems impinge on efficiency. Custody visitors can assist the custody officer by bypassing internal bureaucratic administrative procedures and lobby the right person who can implement immediate action, thereby improving the working environment for custody staff.

In comparison with Her Majesty's Prison (HMP) service, little has been researched and published in relation to the prevention of deliberate self-harm and suicide in police custody in the United Kingdom, although that unsatisfactory situation is changing. HMP has a research unit situated in London (http://pso.hmprisonservice.gov.uk/PSO_2700_suicide_and_self_harm_prevention.doc) that undertakes that task and disseminates key information and good practice. It should be noted, of course, that HMP is a centralised organisation, unlike the structure of the British police service, although in recent years the Association of Chief Police Officers (ACPO) has addressed this issue, which remains a key priority for all custody staff.

One of the first indications that this issue of self-harm and suicide in police custody was being researched was the publication, in May 1997, of the results of a study conducted by two Lancashire constabulary inspectors, Alan Ingram and Graham Johnson, and a principal prison officer, Ian Heyes, from HMP Garth. The results of this study, to some of which we now turn, were extremely revealing and laid the foundation for further development, and the police service overall owes them a debt of gratitude. In a wide-ranging report that looks at both incidents of deaths in custody and deliberate self-harm, several revealing facts justify further analysis and comment here.

First, the authors analysed 52 deaths in police custody from deliberate self-harm, that is, self-inflicted between the years 1990 and 1995. In respect of the *timings* of these incidents, 13 per cent occurred within the first hour and 48 per cent within six hours. Consequently, 61 per cent of the incidents studied occurred within the first six hours, or up to the time of the first detention review by an inspector, following the initial detention being authorised by the custody officer (Ingram et al., 1997, p 17). This indicated that the early part of detention was a crucial period and arguably when a vulnerable person was most at risk. Consider what was asked in the reflective task earlier regarding feeling 'anxious' when first brought into a police custody facility.

Second, in respect of the main *causes* of the incidents, all the cases examined were as a result of hanging, self-strangulation or suspension. However, in 38 per cent of the cases examined, this was facilitated by a prisoner attaching a suitable ligature to an open hatch fitted in a cell door. The issue of hatches in cell doors has been around for some years. The first reference to it was in 1968 when the Home Office circulated Home Office Circular No: 92/1968 drawing the attention of the police forces to the potential opportunities for self-harm via cell door hinges and hatches (Ingram et al., 1997). The situation is improving regarding cell doors, and the older traditional designs are being replaced with modern purpose-built specifications installed keeping the *prevention* of self-harm as paramount (Personal Interview: Merseyside Police, Force Custody Unit, February 2011).

---

**PRACTICAL TASK**

*Go to the website provided below, navigate the site and peruse the designs on offer. Having done so, answer the following question.*

- *What do the design of the cell doors provide the means for custody officers to do?*

*www.cellsecurity.co.uk/shop/catalog/cell-prison-doors-c-21.html*

*Before we conclude this analysis of the prevention of self-harm and suicide in police custody, it is prudent to add that since the pioneering work of Ingram et al., (1997) other developments have occurred. Her Majesty's Inspector of Constabulary, together with Her Majesty's Inspector of Prisons, has commenced a programme of joint visits to police custody facilities. See the website provided below which contains the inspection reports of custody facilities inspected to date. Some are very robust in their findings.*

*www.hmic.gov.uk/INSPECTIONS/JOINTINSPECTIONS/Pages/Joint InspectionofPoliceCustodyFacilities.aspx*

*Furthermore and perhaps more poignantly, in 2006 a document sponsored by ACPO entitled 'Safer Detention and the Handling of Persons in Police Custody' was published primarily aimed at the training of custody staff. See the website given below, where a copy of this document can be accessed.*

*http://saferdetention.co.uk/latest-legislation-and-codes/i/64*

---

To some, this key function and responsibility of the custody officer appears onerous and certainly cannot be underestimated. Provided, procedures are strictly followed and the custody team works together and proactively, regrettable incidents can be kept to an absolute minimum at worst and eliminated totally at best. To achieve that situation a pivotal custody staff member is the detention officer.

# Detention officer

The role of the detention officer or civilian custody assistant, as it is referred to in some forces, is a million miles from the 'turnkey' image that it may portray.

The custody suite is equipped with numerous information technology systems these days which are mainly used by the detention officers. For example, the 'Live Scan' machine, housed in custody suites is used for the electronic scanning of fingerprints and palm-prints and provides a direct link to the national database. Consequently, fingerprints need to be of a good quality. Detention officers, as they use this facility regularly, compared to some operational officers, normally fulfil this requirement.

Prior to the inception of civilian detention officers, the role was performed by police officers who were often rotated around different duties. Hence, expertise was in short supply. The introduction of detention officers addressed that situation and most are employed directly by police authorities or work for contracted security companies. The custody officer is always a police officer. However, detention officers become the 'eyes and ears' of the custody officer, or put another way, the 'radar and sonar' – such is the crucial role that they perform in detecting potential risks, as can be seen from the previous section of this chapter.

One of the key functions in respect of the prevention of self-harm and also protection of injury to the custody staff is the thorough, but ethical, searching of prisoners when first received at the custody suite. Detention officers develop key skills in this area and on many occasions have proved their skills to be more finely toned to those of operational police officers.

Visiting detainees in their cells is obviously a primary role of the detention officer, and these visits are recorded on the custody record.

Again, like custody visitors, experienced detention officers develop skills to look for indicators for potential at-risk prisoners, including those suffering from mental disorder. Often prisoners, who are brought to the custody suite upset and uncooperative with the arresting police officers, behave completely passively with the detention officers, recognising that they are there for their care and welfare, as opposed to gathering evidence against them for a potential prosecution. Good detention officers will identify with this and develop a rapport which procures the co-operation of the detainee, based on good communication skills, crucial for the smooth operational running of the custody suite. These skills come into play throughout a detention officer's role, given the amount of professional visitors to the custody suite, such as solicitors and social workers acting as appropriate adults for detainees, in addition to the number of telephone calls received from concerned family members. Custody staff need to be skilled at dealing with people from all walks of life in a professional manner. Moreover, most visits by independent custody visitors are hosted by detention officers, acting on behalf of the custody officer.

Not all prisoners are co-operative and many may be under the influence of alcohol. In these circumstances, tact and diplomacy is needed while not losing sight of the potential tragic circumstances that could occur with a drunken prisoner. Here again diligence and proactivity is required. Prisoners under the influence of alcohol are normally visited and roused every 30 minutes while they are in custody and are housed in specially adapted cells.

Furthermore, to assist communication *between* detention officers, informal systems such as portable and adhesive signs for use on cell doors containing a red letter 'R' have been introduced (Personal Interview: Merseyside Police, Force Custody Unit, February 2011).

Hygiene is particularly crucial within a custody suite and as well as washing and showering facilities being available for prisoners under the supervision of the detention officers; food preparation for consumption by detainees is the responsibility of detention officers. Under PACE, prisoners are entitled to one main meal and two light meals on a daily basis and at set intervals. Therefore, this is a key role and one that is often scrutinised by independent custody visitors. Most detention officers complete a certificate in food hygiene during their custody training.

This is a diverse role, incorporating a number of key and technical skills and one that should not be undervalued, particularly as it continues to develop within the technological age.

## Case management officer

In an adversarial criminal justice system (CJS) such as the English and Welsh system, the burden of proof in a criminal trial rests with the prosecution. As a consequence, it is vital that evidence is fully and properly presented in court. This requires professional expertise.

As Chapter 4 of this book indicates, the miscarriages of justice highlighted significant problems with the CJS. Furthermore, over the past 30 years, the status of the victim has become more of a key issue within the CJS following the overall plight being highlighted by several academic sources (Christie, 1977 in McLaughlin et al., 2003). Therefore, several issues coalesced and a number of initiatives have been implemented in the last few years aimed at ameliorating and restoring public confidence in the system. For example, the Local Criminal Justice Boards have been introduced, structured broadly on the boundaries of police forces in England and Wales.

---

PRACTICAL TASK

*Go to the following website, access frequently asked questions and answer the following.*

- *What is the Local Criminal Justice Board?*

*http://lcjb.cjsonline.gov.uk/Merseyside/home.html*

---

The decision to charge a detainee has always rested with the custody officer. However, in the last few years, the government, via the CPS, has introduced a revised system called the Statutory Charging Scheme. Basically, in the most minor of cases, before charging, the case must be referred to the CPS for a decision. Currently, the police only decide the charge in the most minor of cases or cases where there has been a formal admission and a guilty plea is anticipated (Personal Interview: Merseyside Police, Force Custody Unit, February 2011). In all matters, it must be referred to the CPS.

---

*REFLECTIVE TASK*

*Go to the following website and answer the following.*

*www.cps.gov.uk/about/charging.html*

- *What has the 'Prosecution Team' approach managed to achieve?*
- *Who is it providing a better service to?*
- *What is perceived to be the 'most significant development' since the inception of the CPS?*
- *List your reasons why you think that is.*

---

Clearly, a key element of the 'Prosecution Team' is the case management officer (CMO), and in some forces they are referred to as the Evidence Review Officer, or more colloquially the 'gate keeper' – which accurately summarises their primary role. Normally based within the custody suite area the CMO is the first interface between the CPS and the police.

Generally, it is an experienced sergeant or detective sergeant who undertakes this role, and somebody with ample experience either as a custody officer or working within a police unit responsible for case preparation. Unlike the custody officer who must remain independent of the investigation, it is the role of the CMO to give advice on it.

A mandatory skill that a CMO must possess is the ability to forensically assess written evidence from victims, witnesses and police officers and make a judgement based on legal knowledge, as to whether an arrest at the custody suite is evidentially sufficiently robust for submission to the CPS.

As indicated earlier, it is the CPS who decide about charging and subsequent process within the CJS. Another requirement is good organisational skills and time management. Although prosecution files are submitted electronically either via NSIPS or Niche RMS to the CPS, thereby avoiding reams of paper or bulky files that can go astray, this process begins at the custody suite when the prisoner is first received into custody.

Perhaps, like the detention officer, communication is the most important skill for a CMO. It is crucial to be able to confidently discuss evidential matters at the right level, with all users of the custody suite, from newly appointed probationary police officers to experienced criminal advocates reviewing cases for the CPS.

Prosecution files and also files submitted for advice only must be in a specified format and meet certain standards in respect of quality and timeliness. The CMO must ensure that these requirements are met before further transmission to the CPS; hence, the sobriquet 'gate keeper' which is a crucial and pivotal role in the contemporary police service.

**C H A P T E R   S U M M A R Y**

This chapter provides a broad overview of the roles and some of the duties of the custody officer, detention officer and CMO.

It also highlights how the role of custody officer has evolved and why, illustrating some of the reasons for this and statutory requirements placed upon police officers in this regard. A key theme running throughout the chapter is the need for professionalism in all aspects of operational custody provision, in an area of police work that has historically been often undervalued and somewhat disregarded as incidental, to one which is slowly, but finally developing into a respected specialism.

---

**CASE STUDY**

*As we discussed in the chapter, the first knowledge the custody staff are likely to have of the robbery at Roman's Newsagent, High Street will be a telephone call from the control room enquiring if the custody suite can accept persons who have been arrested for the offence. In itself it appears a straightforward request; however, like any other establishment that offers accommodation (secure or otherwise), the custody suite can and often does become full to capacity where there are 'no vacancies'. If this was the case, then those detained would be taken to an alternative custody suite.*

*In this case study, where more than one person is arrested, it is often common practice to take the detainees to separate custody suites, if practicable. In rural areas, where custody suites are allocated on a county-by-county basis, such as West Mercia Police, this may not be feasible. The reasons for doing this are fairly obvious. It prevents the opportunity for offender collusion in the cell areas and is also good practice in relation to the prevention of forensic contamination. However, in this case, both offenders are brought to the same suite.*

*On arrival at the custody suite, those under arrest entered the holding area accompanied by the police officers who made the arrest. This is an ante-room to the custody suite and the access to the suite is controlled by the custody staff. This is to prevent overcrowding in the custody desk area, which is occupied by the custody officer and detention staff.*

*Having been granted access, the circumstances of the arrest were relayed to the custody officer by the arresting police officer. The custody officer then made the decision that the reasons for the arrest and detention were valid and as such, authorised detention accordingly and told them of their individual rights under PACE. With the detention authorised, the custody records were opened for both detainees.*

*They were then searched by the arresting officer and their property (such as money, jewellery and watches) recorded on the custody record. The relevant checks were carried out via the PNC to see, for example, if they were wanted elsewhere in the country for an offence, and both individuals were placed in separate cells in the male cell area.*

*During the early stages of their detention in the custody suite, both detainees had their photographs, DNA and fingerprints taken by the detention officers. If forensic samples were required, such as the seizing of their shoes for comparison against the footwear marks found at the crime scene, then this would be entered on the custody record. The investigation team would also need to consider if their clothing is to be seized for forensic purposes. If so, the detainees would be provided with alternative clothing for use within the custody suite. As fibres were found at the crime scene, the outer clothing was seized.*

*They may also be seen by the FME if further intimate samples, such as a dental impression (although not in this case), were to be taken from those in custody. This, of course, is in addition to any medical screening in relation to fitness for interview or custody that may be taken.*

*In this case, the detainees also requested the appointment of a solicitor and asked to consult with their legal advisor confidentially, through telephone at first, and then in person before commencing the interview by the police detective.*

*The initial stages of dealing with the offence of a robbery has led to an effective team, with numerous specialisms, identifying and arresting two individuals who were detained in custody. Evidence, in the form of statements collected from witnesses, police officers and police staff involved, physical evidence collected from the crime scene, along with effective interviewing by police detectives will lead to the eventual proving, or otherwise, of the involvement of those detained in the commission of the crime.*

# Self-assessment questions

1.  Which Act of Parliament created the custody officer?

2.  What must a custody officer remain independent of?

3. What does a custody officer authorise following an arrest?

4. What does NSPIS stand for?

5. What is 'Livescan' used for?

6. Are all prisoners co-operative?

7. What is the title given to independent persons appointed by the Police Authority to visit prisoners in police custody?

8. Who first recommended this scheme?

9. What must detention officers do when visiting drunken prisoners?

10. The CMO is also known as what?

**REFERENCES**

Blake, C, Sheldon, B and Williams, P (2010) *Policing and Criminal Justice*. Exeter: Learning Matters.

Ingram, A, Johnson, G and Heyes, I (1997) *Self Harm and Suicide by Detained Persons: A Study*. Police Research Award. Police Research Group. London: Home Office.

McLaughlin, E, Fergusson, R, Hughes, G and Westmarland, L (2003) *Restorative Justice Critical Issues*. London: Sage.

Personal Interview: Sergeant Christopher Lee, Merseyside Police, Force Custody Unit. February, 2011.

Police Product Review (February/March 2011) *Jane's Police Product Review*, 42. London: James Green.

Williams, P (2005) 'Are the Blue Boys the Original Boys in Blue?' *Journal of the Police History Society*. 20.

**USEFUL WEBSITES**

http://hansard.millbanksystems.com/commons/1977/dec/12/mr-liddle-towers (accessed 23 March 2011).

http://pso.hmprisonservice.gov.uk/PSO_2700_suicide_and_self_harm_prevention.doc (accessed 23 March 2011).

www.britishlistedbuildings.co.uk/en-213886-main-bridewell-liverpool (accessed 24 March 2011).

www.cps.gov.uk/about/charging.html (accessed 20 March 2011).

www.cps.gov.uk/about/history.html (accessed 20 March 2011).

www.fomphc.org.uk/faq.php?cat_id=8&rowstart=30 (accessed 23 March 2011).

www.mpa.gov.uk/committees/x-cdo/2000/000926/14/ (accessed 3 March 2011).

www.cellsecurity.co.uk/shop/catalog/cell-prison-doors-c-21.html (accessed 24 March 2011).

www.hmic.gov.uk/INSPECTIONS/JOINTINSPECTIONS/Pages/JointInspectionofPoliceCustodyFacilities.aspx (accessed 23 March 2011).

http://saferdetention.co.uk/latest-legislation-and-codes/i/64 (accessed 23 March 2011).

http://lcjb.cjsonline.gov.uk/Merseyside/home.html (accessed 3 March 2011).

# Appendix: police services websites

## Police forces across England and Wales

| Force name | Force website |
|---|---|
| Avon and Somerset Constabulary | www.avonandsomerset.police.uk/ |
| Bedfordshire Police | www.bedfordshire.police.uk/ |
| Cambridgeshire Constabulary | www.cambs.police.uk/ |
| Cheshire Constabulary | www.cheshire.police.uk/ |
| City of London Police | www.cityoflondon.police.uk/citypolice/ |
| Cleveland Police | www.cleveland.police.uk/ |
| Cumbria Constabulary | www.cumbria.police.uk/ |
| Derbyshire Constabulary | www.derbyshire.police.uk/ |
| Devon and Cornwall Police | www.devon-cornwall.police.uk/ |
| Dorset Police | www.dorset.police.uk/ |
| Durham Constabulary | www.durham.police.uk/ |
| Dyfed-Powys Police | www.dyfed-powys.police.uk/en/ |
| Essex Police | www.essex.police.uk/ |
| Gloucestershire Constabulary | www.gloucestershire.police.uk/ |
| Greater Manchester Police | www.gmp.police.uk/ |
| Gwent Police | www.gwent.police.uk/ |
| Hampshire Constabulary | www.hampshire.police.uk/ |
| Hertfordshire Constabulary | www.herts.police.uk/ |
| Humberside Police | www.humberside.police.uk/ |
| Kent Police | www.kent.police.uk/ |
| Lancashire Constabulary | www.lancashire.police.uk/ |
| Leicestershire Constabulary | www.leics.police.uk/ |
| Lincolnshire Police | www.lincs.police.uk/ |
| Merseyside Police | www.merseyside.police.uk/ |
| Metropolitan Police Service | www.met.police.uk/ |
| Norfolk Constabulary | www.norfolk.police.uk/ |
| North Wales Police | www.north-wales.police.uk/ |
| North Yorkshire Police | www.northyorkshire.police.uk/ |
| Northamptonshire Police | www.northants.police.uk/ |

| | |
|---|---|
| Northumbria Police | www.northumbria.police.uk/ |
| Nottinghamshire Police | www.nottinghamshire.police.uk/ |
| South Wales Police | www.south-wales.police.uk/ |
| South Yorkshire Police | www.southyorks.police.uk/ |
| Staffordshire Police | www.staffordshire.police.uk/ |
| Suffolk Constabulary | www.suffolk.police.uk/ |
| Surrey Police | www.surrey.police.uk/ |
| Sussex Police | www.sussex.police.uk/ |
| Thames Valley Police | www.thamesvalley.police.uk/ |
| Warwickshire Police | www.warwickshire.police.uk/ |
| West Mercia Police | www.westmercia.police.uk/ |
| West Midlands Police | www.west-midlands.police.uk/ |
| West Yorkshire Police | www.westyorkshire.police.uk/ |
| Wiltshire Constabulary | www.wiltshire.police.uk/ |

# Police Forces across Scotland

| Force name | Force website |
|---|---|
| Central Scotland Police | www.centralscotland.police.uk/ |
| Dumfries and Galloway Constabulary | www.dumfriesandgalloway.police.uk/ |
| Fife Constabulary | www.fife.police.uk/ |
| Grampian Police | www.grampian.police.uk/ |
| Lothian and Borders Police | www.lbp.police.uk/ |
| Northern Constabulary | www.northern.police.uk/ |
| Strathclyde Police | www.strathclyde.police.uk/ |
| Tayside Police | www.tayside.police.uk/ |

# Northern Ireland

| Force name | Force website |
|---|---|
| Police Service of Northern Ireland (PSNI) | www.psni.police.uk/ |

# Other police forces across the United Kingdom and associated territories

| Force name | Force website |
| --- | --- |
| Bermuda Police Service | www.bermudapolice.bm/ |
| British Transport Police | www.btp.police.uk/ |
| Civil Nuclear Constabulary | www.cnc.police.uk/ |
| Guernsey Police | www.guernsey.police.uk/ |
| Isle of Man Constabulary | www.gov.im/dha/police/ |
| Ministry of Defence Police | www.mod.police.uk/ |
| National Police Improvement Agency (NPIA) | www.npia.police.uk/ |
| Royal Air Force Police (RAFP) | www.raf.mod.uk/careers/jobs/ |
| Royal Cayman Islands Police Service | www.rcips.ky/ |
| Royal Falkland Islands Police | www.falklands.gov.fk/Police/ |
| Royal Gibraltar Police | www.gibraltar.gov.gi/royal-gibraltar-police/ |
| Royal Military Police (RMP) | www.army.mod.uk/join/ |
| Royal Navy Police (RNP) | www.royalnavy.mod.uk/careers/ |
| Royal Virgin Islands Police Force | www.rvipolice.com/ |
| Scottish Drug Enforcement Agency | www.sdea.police.uk/ |
| Scottish Police College | http://tulliallan.police.uk/ |
| Serious and Organised Crime Agency (SOCA) | www.soca.gov.uk/ |
| Sovereign Base Areas Police, Cyprus | www.sba.mod.uk/ |
| States of Jersey Police | www.jersey.police.uk/ |
| St. Helena Police Department | www.sainthelena.gov.sh/ |

# Index